Audit of the Universe

The Explanation, Volume 2

Sam Kneller

Published by Sam Kneller, 2020.

Also by Sam Kneller

The Explanation
Inventory of the Universe
Audit of the Universe
Origin of the Universe
Origin of Humankind
Origin of Woman

Watch for more at https://www.TheExplanation.com.

Table of Contents

Proprietorship

---

1. http://www.TheExplanation.com

Preface

It's time to take a look at the state of affairs of our *Inventory of the Universe*. What is humankind's impact on our planet Earth and beyond?

If you have followed our travelers from *Inventory of the Universe*, Volume I of *The Explanation*, you are no doubt ready for a brief relaxing pause before embarking on the journey of the state of affairs of our surroundings in the pages that follow.

Majestic Nature

We'll begin our interlude with a little foray into nature, as I chat with Galacti. "The other night, I happened on a TV program about migrating birds and a must-stop on their South to North flight, in Eilat, Israel.

There, Good Samaritans are trying to provide a haven for the birds, after a 1500 to 3000 km journey across a foodless, waterless, harsh, searing and unforgiving Sahara Desert.

The documentary panned over majestic eagles waiting for the sun to allow the desert heat to create thermal updrafts, then circling effortlessly as the warm air helps them ascend so high they can't be seen by the naked eye. Then, gliding for miles and miles until they zero in on another thermal, which again whisks them aloft into the altitudes. Powerful birds are barely batting their wings, saving energy, using nature, covering some 300 km per day.

I saw the peregrine falcon, sometimes called the duck hawk, using convection currents to rise into the gulf stream air passage and travel at over 300km per hour! Structurally the bird has to have wings, muscles, lungs, and metabolism, down to the last detail, all engineered for this dangerous mission.

The same program pointed out how bird watching has soared to new heights through emitters attached harmlessly to these flying wonders. Equipped with GPS, movement measurement, memory, and sophisticated transmission, the devices make it possible to know where the birds are and what they're doing every ten minutes. Reams of data for tracking purposes useful, amongst other things, during concentrated migration periods, as birds can be a substantial threat to aviation."

Galacti nods in agreement as I talk about the wonder of nature and technology, the natural world and human know-how, the clash or concord of Earth's environment, and human-made equipment.

Ponder the pride of majestic lions that sleep 20 hours a day and siafu ants traveling in colonies of 20 million, with jaws so strong, that in emergency medical circumstances, they have been used to replace stitches to close a wound; these are instinctive killers. Yet, they only stake out the territory they need; they've never taken over a neighbor-hood, let alone a country. In the natural habitat, there's always equilibrium.

Not so, when we introduce the Human equation.

Today, as never before, with a world population expanding exponentially, wherever humankind steps, it leaves its trace, even managing to turn majestic **Mount Everest into a garbage dump**. What is our planetary environmental state of affairs?

In *Inventory of the Universe,* we turned over all the pieces of the puzzle, from A (atmosphere) to Z (zoology), from the most massive most impenetrable galaxies in the universe to the minutest now confirmed Higgs Boson particle, revealed by the LHC particle accelerator in Switzerland. From the inorganic minerals to flora and fauna life, down to Humankind's body and mind. We opened our eyes to survey our incredible inventory.

Together on our odyssey, we travelers have completed the inventory, and although it's a hostile place outside of the Earth's atmosphere, we agree that it's spectacular and enticing. That for us humans, the air we breathe and the water we drink are just right for our needs. Earth is a very hospitable place to live, providing us with all the greenery and animals we could ever need for our sustenance, development, enjoyment, and wonderment.

Yes, we have all the pieces to do with our universe; we know with which parts we must work. It's time to see the interplay between these pieces. The impact of one on the other, with a particular emphasis on humankind's role, after all, by whatever design, humanity is the main instigator on this planet. We have to take a look at our effect on our environment.

Galacti wants to know: What is the state of affairs?

Some readers may be wondering: how do we decide? What are our criteria? Fair warning: yes, this is going to be subjective. We have only so much space so that we can include only so many examples; I have to make a choice. On the other hand, that's also the reason I've decided to self-publish this work, allowing for ongoing edits and additions as well as using the power and unlimited memory of the internet to be able to include reader contributions.

As people are more and more mobile and information shoots around the globe, it accumulates and is shaped, interpreted, and edited on websites and apps. Likewise, the state of affairs of our planet is anything but immobile; it evolves each day all around the world.

Therefore, *The Explanation* welcomes creative, constructive contributions or articles and references to other works to enhance comprehension of all the pieces of the puzzle. A combined input of reliable information from various sources brings us a better awareness of what the state of our planet really is.

In browsing social media and in talking to people in my travels, I find everybody believes there are both wondrous and awful events going on simultaneously around us; that the proverbial glass is both half full and half empty. The squabbling is over the tendency: is it getting fuller or emptier? Are we getting better-off or worse-off? In this argument, we can and do use statistics, observations, and examples to push home our cases. They might be objective facts, but when we dress them with our feelings, that's where subjectivity enters the scene.

And where there's subjectivity, there's divergence and discord, "your ideas are as good as mine." And the deceptive adage "there's no right or wrong." Enter conflict, controversy, and tension, which can lead to ill feelings, outright hostility, and rigid extremism.

But, on the other hand, can anyone stay *neutral*? My opinion is that there's some good, some bad. Some would say it's always been that way, and we're going to continue like that ad infinitum. That is a way of looking at it, but it's a cop-out; after all, you know whether you're drinking from or pouring your favorite beverage into the glass.

Likewise, in Volume 2, *Audit of the Universe*, we'll see the tendency of the glass, getting fuller or emptier. Also with Volume 3, *Audit of Humankind*[1]. Some readers will agree, others will disagree, so what I'd like to say here is this. Starting with Volume 4, *Origin of the Universe*[2], I'll explain WHY the glass has the tendency it does, and in Volume 5, *Origin of Humankind*[3], what humanity's role is with a focus on the male gender and the human mind. Volume 6, *Origin of Woman*[4] is the surprising story of, In the garden with our Mother, the first Woman. Volume 7, *Agony of Humankind and the Antidote*[5] explains the why of today's worldwide state of affairs and how to turn the situation around. The purpose of *The Explanation* is to put the whole puzzle together.

Evaluating where we are at the beginning of the 21st century is an *Audit of the Universe*, an assessment of the relationship of Earth to its inhabitants. It does not yet explain how Earth got that way, why it is that way, or where Earth and humankind are going from there. It is merely a spot check. But, to give *The Explanation* of the how, why, and where, we must first assess the state of affairs of our inventory.

Let's begin our audit of the universe.

---

1. https://theexplanation.com/read-all-the-content-of-audit-of-humankind-online/

2. https://theexplanation.com/read-content-origin-universe-online/

3. https://theexplanation.com/read-content-origin-humankind-online/

4. https://theexplanation.com/read-all-the-content-of-origin-of-woman-online/

5. https://theexplanation.com/read-all-the-content-of-agony-of-humankind-online/

Housekeeping Issues

Some links in this e-book connect you to websites on the Internet. Hence the need for an internet connection as you read. That said, the subject is understandable without navigating to those links. All links were correct at the time of publication. If you find an issue, let me know at sam@theexplanation.com. Thanks in advance.

During your read, you'll meet *Galacti,* who is our fictitious time-traveling, investigative, roving reporter who lends his insights and voice to the development of the narrative of this e-book and *The Explanation.*

If you've come across this e-book for the first time, then please know that it is part of a much larger work: *The Explanation* series. See all the books and the entire context[1].

https://TheExplanation.com

Join The Explanation Newsletter[2], no spam, total privacy. Receive Sam's latest blog post notifications and information about *The Explanation*

---

1. https://theexplanation.com/the-explanation-books-to-buy/

2. https://mailchi.mp/theexplanation/7keystomasterbiblicalhebrew

1. Audit of Space

Nuclear Power and Waste

Nuclear power, a dilemma of the 21st century, has become one of the major controversies of the 21st century—clean, cheap power versus dangerous waste and possible accidents. The issues are many, and the stakes are high.

"Imagine the unimaginable." Galacti intones the phrase.

We stand on the spot where we first touched down in _Inventory of the Universe_ Chapter 2[1] when we journeyed through the atmosphere. The night is so black we see only the vague outlines of trees and perhaps a house or two nearby, with the faint glow of electric light in the windows. House lights cannot compete with the sight above our heads.

The starry sky beckons our gaze. There is no light pollution where we are so that we can see the star-filled pavilion in its entirety. There are no clouds—however, clouds of gas play a role in the formation of the star spectacle that entrances us.

No wonder Carl Sagan said that "... _the total number of stars in the universe is greater than all the grains of sand on all the beaches of the planet Earth._" The number of objects in the universe is mind-boggling—estimated at 10 trillion galaxies, each with 100 billion stars—that's one followed by 24 zeroes.

Observing the stars and planets and thinking about baby stars being born right now as we stand here leads us to ponder: what more is out there? Gazing up at the stars has led humankind to expand its knowledge outward as we explore the universe with the tools we create, and inward, as our minds think about the possibilities of life

By now, we are used to these moments of considering what was right under our noses. Or, above them in this case, and have learned to expect the unpredictable.

Before we can proceed with a plan to understand the why of the origin of Earth and humankind, we need to know where we are. What's going well? What's going wrong? What needs tweaking? What needs a makeover or total replacement?

---

1. http://theexplanation.com/earths-atmosphere-ingredients-life/

We're going to do an audit, starting with the atom. We're starting another journey with Galacti filled with real-life examples to help us analyze and even decide whether the half-empty/half-full glass is getting emptier or fuller.

Atomic Power and Earthquakes

We have seen the atomic and subatomic level—but atomic and nuclear power forces are at work every day, in minute and large-scale ways. The following three stories presented by Galacti will invite us to explore this topic.

The idea of nuclear power evokes everything from awe to images of *mushroom clouds* as well as the atom bombs dropped on **Hiroshima with the ensuing destruction of the *Atomic Dome*.**

Galacti is quick to point out that Japan shut down 52 of its 54 nuclear reactors following the meltdowns at Fukushima-Daiichi.

Also, Russia has harnessed atomic power to transport liquefied natural gas from Norway to Japan via the Arctic/Northern Sea Route—through the ice. In this story, a Greek-operated carrier shipping the clean natural gas follows three Russian atomic icebreakers that embark from the Norwegian port of Hammerfest and cut swaths through the ice of the Bering Strait.

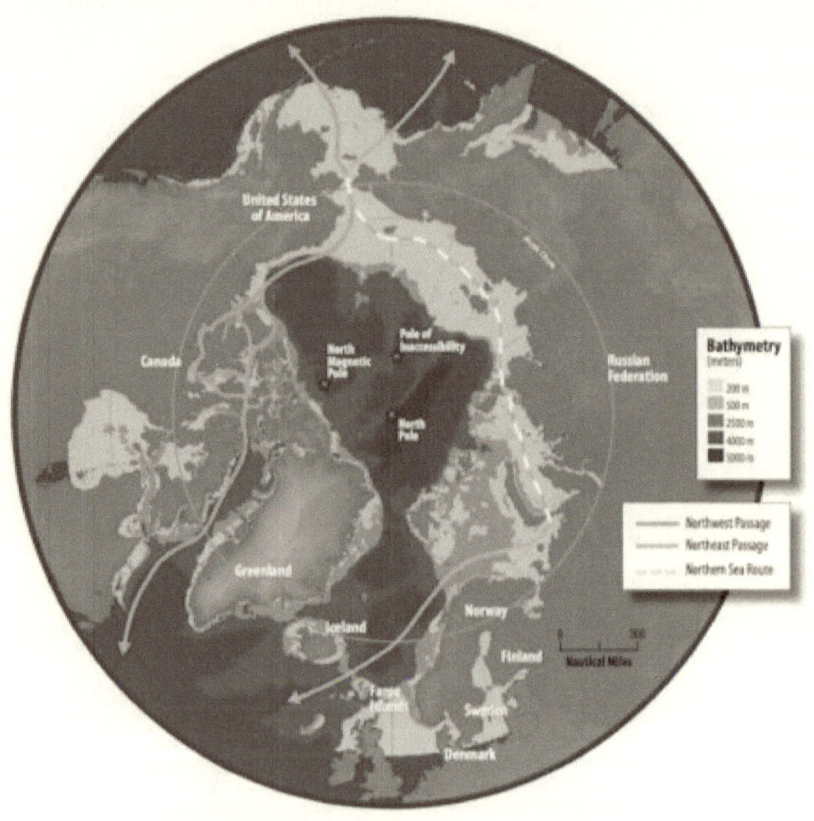

The route, shorter than the traditional southern shipping lanes through the Suez Canal, **saves fuel and reduces pollution, all of this is possible thanks to atomic power, to the small reactors, 52 kilograms** (114 pounds), the size of a female Japanese judo champion, that power the icebreakers.

Galacti and our tour group find **both a negative and positive aspect to nuclear energy**: the bombing of cities, meltdown, contamination and the powerful icebreakers which are helping to supply the natural gas Japan has been relying on ever since the nuclear power

Imagine a string of earthquakes 4.5 and above on the Richter triggering a nuclear meltdown in Rajasthan, India or Laguna Verde, Mexico, or Angra, Brazil. If you are in such *earth-shattering* events, you may not think to ask, "By the way, is there a nuclear power plant in the neighboring country? How many? How many under construction?"

We've heard of the Chernobyl disaster and the tsunami/earthquake (8.9 on the Richter) that triggered the meltdown at Fukushima-Daiichi. But seismic activity in the region's surrounding locations, with one or more active nuclear reactors as well as ones under construction, seems like a scene out of a James Bond movie. However, with North Korea's September 2016 nuclear test triggering a 5.3 earthquake[2], citizens around the globe have taken notice.

Nuclear Waste Buried

German protesters converge on a nuclear waste storage site in Gorleben, Germany. The atomic dump is notorious, with its tunnels closed off, as a sign in red German letters warns. This facility contains barrels of toxic radioactive waste such as irradiated nuclear reactor fuel, liquid, and solid waste byproducts, nuclei formed by the fission of heavy elements.

---

2. https://www.bbc.com/news/world-asia-21421841

Protesters from all over the world, whose voices are amplified by news reports from CNN and the BBC, protested this train at its point of origin in France and the Gorleben facility. The train's nuclear containers, massive white hulks containing 123 tons of spent fuel, carry the dangerous waste to the abandoned mine in Gorleben. One Greenpeace scientist measures the radiation at about 4,000 counts per minute or the same level as Chernobyl. At the same time, trains will carry spent fuel for reprocessing from East Germany to a facility in Russia.

Hundreds of anti-nuclear protesters lie on the tracks in an attempt to stop the train from reaching the *temporary dump*. The abandoned mine facility is the closest solution to a high-level repository for nuclear waste. None of the 31 countries that have nuclear power plants, or the 45 countries considering atomic power, possesses an advanced nuclear waste storage facility.

The Gorleben mine site or the hotly contested Yucca Mountain site in the U.S. are the most advanced solutions humankind has yet proposed. Gorleben is only a temporary storage site, and as of this, writing still awaits its ultimate destiny.

International peace teams believe that the Gorleben radioactive waste is a threat to safety and liberty. Already international groups note that, inside a similarly converted salt mine now serving as a storage facility, radioactive brine has been leaking into the ground for two decades. And there are severe doubts about the viability of the long-term salt mine storage.

There are questions about preserving the metallic, off-white, or yellow silo-like **containers of nuclear wastes. These CASTORS are** *casks for storage and transport of radioactive material* that may be destroyed by salt since geological drillings have proved the salt, where they're stored, is unstable, and cause leakage long-term. Already policymakers in India are pointing to Gorleben as a sign that India should not rush to expand its nuclear program.

We leave off this *hot topic* since there is much more to explore on the subject of atoms and in the realm of space.

Sun, Moon, Stars - Grandiose

From atoms to astral bodies: sun, moon, stars. They light up our sky, and both awe us and leave us quizzical with their grandeur and mysterious presence.

Navigation - Guiding the Way

Just as we've gently led our travelers on a journey to find all the puzzle pieces—with many more, before we have the complete picture—so **the stars have directed humans to find their way.**

We watch sailors using Ptolemy's maps and then orienting themselves north or south by observing the positions of major **navigational stars**[1]. **The North Star or Polaris**, which we find in the Little Dipper (Ursa Minor) constellation, itself a navigational point, and the Southern Cross that points towards the celestial South Pole.

The North Star never moves, in contrast to the stars around it, so that it is a fixed point for seafarers to determine their latitude; in fact, **no matter what your position, you can view the North Star at the same angle in relation to the horizon.** It's our directional beacon.

Someone uses a GPS to read our latitude. In centuries past, he might have used an astrolabe, a spherical handheld analog calculator, that contains a moving disk to represent the position of the stars. Or a cross-staff, which uses several *vanes* or slats sliding on a central staff to measure the angles between stars, and the height of the Pole Star and the sun.

Galacti has produced replicas of these, as well as the back-staff, a device outfitted with mirrors so that when we look through the sight vane, with the top *lens* or vane reminding us of a submarine periscope, we can see Polaris. In the daytime, we can view the Sun without any harm to our eyes.

Look at the GPS, with its easy digital readout, and compare it with the ancient navigation tools. Both are obviously of human origin, but very different. **The GPS doesn't use the stars in any way to determine our latitude.** So, you might think. But consider this: a satellite and this computer receiver have replaced the astrolabe and the back-staff.

We all agree this is something to consider. We've never really thought about this. Likewise, we give little thought to something else the sun, moon, and stars have provided us with: **the calendar.**

---

1. https://en.wikipedia.org/wiki/List_of_stars_for_navigation

We have discussed the seasons, which man could observe unaided without calculation. The calendar, however, is another matter. While we can't watch the orbits of the Earth and Moon to count days, we now know that it takes 365 days for the Earth to complete its orbit around the sun.

However, imagine that we are ancient Chinese, Babylonians, Hebrews or Greeks. While we observe the change of the seasons, we watch the phases of the moon[2]. The lunar phase cycle is 29.5 days or a month, and during our accelerated month, we observe two full moons. We soon discover, however, that there is no fixed number of days in a month, unlike the **solar calendar**.

Also, we learn that a **lunar calendar year is thirteen months** to match the seasons, in particular the harvests. Ancient farmers needed the moon, as well as the solar calendar, to tell them when to plant and when to harvest. Also, the phases of the moon are associated with specific festivals and celebrations of the passage of life. While this may sound complicated, the lunar months are still part of the Jewish calendar; each month begins on the New Moon.

Imagine living by the lunar calendar, and **performing astronomical calculations to mark the passage of months** (as the Egyptians did), and **marking religious observances and agricultural cycles** by the phases of the moon. Our observers talk about stories and beliefs they've heard about the moon, stars, and sun, dating back to ancient times.

Worship - Good and Bad Omens

"You humans believe in good or bad omens," Galacti says, shaking his head, "I've been reading up on it, accessing the library of the universe. You've seen the composition of a star and the Big Bang. **Who can honestly tell me you believe in omens or *divine favors* as you call them?**

---

2. https://theexplanation.com/day-4-of-creation-sun-and-moon-establish-calendar/

Seeing a halo around the sun and believing it foretells rain? Wishing upon a shooting star, for example? Anyone here from Chile?" A woman who admired our South American plants in *Inventory of the Universe*[3] raises her hand. "It's said that if you see a shooting star in Chile, you will have a year of good luck."

This lady from Chile has heard this tale but never given it much thought.

We all pause to consider the **cultural omens and stories we learned.** For example, the positions of stars and lunar eclipses often herald the birth of a major world figure. We ponder every belief, including the warning that a full moon on Christmas Day will bring bad luck.

The ancient Greeks worshipped meteorites, which they thought represented the stone Zeus' father, Cronos, swallowed instead of Zeus, whom he thought would dethrone him. Many Greek temples enshrined meteorites as objects of worship. Meteorite veneration exists in many cultures on Earth. **Why would a rock from the heavens become something people pray before?**

Planets as well became signs of good luck and the gods. The Babylonians associated Jupiter, Venus, Mercury, Saturn, and Mars with their deities. If Babylonians could read and interpret the motion of the planets, they could understand and predict significant world events. Even the New Moon, which was not associated with any god, was a source of study—if it appeared earlier than expected, cattle or crops would fail and die.

---

3. *https://theexplanation.com/inventory/read-all-the-content-of-inventory-of-the-universe-online/*

The Earth revolves around the sun, which gives the sun a premier place in the universe. The sun[4] is the source of life; it determines the seasons and is essential to life on Earth. That is why it is commonly associated with power, for example, as the Eye of Zeus in Greek mythology. The sun identifies with Egyptian gods, from sun-disks to the solar barge. Japan is called the *Land of The Rising Sun,* and King Louis XIV of France called himself *The Sun King*.

To see the **sunrise at Stonehenge on the winter solstice** signifies that the following year will be a favorable one. Galacti observes that even sun tanning acquires a bit of an exotic mystique, as *sun-worshippers* who deliberately tan are trying to project success, a tropical and desirable lifestyle. Exposure to the sun has many benefits in improving health and mood! In any case, *sun signs* populate the world, most notably in astrology.

---

4. https://www.encyclopedia.com/religion/encyclopedias-almanacs-transcripts-and-maps/astral-religion

Satellites, Eyes on Earth and Us

Thousands of satellites pepper space like eyes in the sky. They survey and scrutinize, some say, spy, on just about everything that takes place on Earth.

Space, both mysterious and hypnotic by its vastness and inaccessibility. Humans have barely penetrated a skinny layer beyond planet Earth. What are we making of this new frontier?

What about the four cardinal points, and how **ancient monuments and megaliths seemingly *mirror* the position of the heavens**? Galacti says as he transports the ancient Irish temple New Grange into the landscape, and next transports Stonehenge several feet away—along the ley lines.

In the new area of archaeological study known as geodesy, **Ley Lines hypothetically link ancient monuments and megaliths.** It fits with the tradition, in many societies, of building prominent structures and historic landmarks according to straight lines.

Think of the Ley Lines as train tracks or a city planned on a grid. **The builders of ancient pyramids in Mexico appear to have designed their structures as if on an axis.** For example: Suppose Stonehenge or La Grange or the Pyramid of Kulkulkan in Chichen Itza in Mexico are the nexus of electrical, magnetic, *mystical* or psychic energy—or landmarks for UFOs to steer by for navigation.

Skeptics and believers put equal faith in disproving or advancing this idea.

Just as you rarely think of ancient navigation aids, you probably don't think of the role the stars still play in navigation today.

Eye on Satellites

Consider that a handful of countries can now blast powerful rockets loaded with satellites into space. A lot of them are in a *geo-stationery* orbit around Earth. At an altitude of 36,000 km, they revolve at the same speed as Earth, always staying in the same position. **Three such satellites can have communications beamed up to and then between them, thus permitting round the world instantaneous verbal, TV, video, web exchanges.** It's brilliant, out of this world.

Just as if you go to the top of a 50-floor skyscraper, you can see further in the distance than if you were on the ground, so, too, **with 120 satellites in the Earth's orbit, every square inch of Earth can be seen and watched**. It's possible to capture the number on a car's license plate as well as monitor military movements, missile launchings, and even self-defense.

Hundreds of other uses like weather forecasting, measuring the height of mountains, the size and topographical changes of the polar caps, and the search for precious elements like lithium for long-life batteries. **Today, thousands of specialized satellites revolve incessantly around in this void,** gathering and transmitting unimaginable amounts of data earthward. But what exactly is that data telling us?

We can view, with the naked eye, one of the global positioning satellites allowing us to pinpoint our location. **There are 24 GPS satellites in orbit, creating a human-made GPS constellation.**

Although we've been traveling using the *Galacti Positioning System*, we're aware of GPS technology during our journey because of our cameras, smartphones, and iPads—all of which use **GPS technology.** Consider that we can speak into our cell phones, or **go to a virtual map and search for whatever it is we want to find—a café au lait, a computer shop, or a planetarium.**

Contrast that with the newborn rats and the navigating monarch butterflies from our zoo filled with ability in *Inventory of the Universe[1]* Section 6 and our human-animal comparison in *Inventory* Section 10. The rats are born knowing where to find food, and butterflies have their own sunlight-activated biological GPS.

Satellites are also conduits for television, radio, cell phones, atmospheric and weather information, and tools to gather and send scientific knowledge, such as data on cosmic X-rays, gamma rays, and electromagnetic radiation back to science centers all over the world.

How do these satellites accumulate and transmit data? **They record *internal data,*** a status report cataloging where the satellites are pointing, whether or not it is functioning, whether the satellite is in danger of colliding with any other object—which admittedly doesn't happen

---

1. *https://theexplanation.com/inventory/read-all-the-content-of-inventory-of-the-universe-online/*

frequently, does it? We might be surprised. In any case, the ground crew regularly checks the satellite's *vital signs* to make sure everything is functioning.

Then we come to the fun part: the images of stars and planets, light spectra, measurements, count rates, and other figures describing Mercury, for example. Fortunately for scientists, **the majority of data the satellites transmit is for our weather stations**. Scientists have two options here: They can wait for a fresh batch of data every orbit or receive the data streamed to them live in realtime.

However, Galacti notes that **the data is only as good as the instruments used.** Hence, it is worth paying attention to the housekeeping data to make sure the devices have the proper calibration. Seeing new dwarf stars, new space phenomena, trying to understand the Big Bang, prompt us to reach farther, to launch the Mars Rovers.

The result of all this satellite technology?

Without being aware of it, we use space as a medium, every day. When we connect to the Internet or make a cell phone call or check the weather before we leave for work or play, we're using satellite signals crisscrossing above the exosphere. Space is not just an idea; space **is part of our everyday lives**—when we look to the heavens and wonder, we also forget that we are using *outer space* to accomplish tasks we all take for granted, with the same confidence with which we have accepted putting a man on the moon.

Mind-boggling.

Also, **via satellite, we can locate sub-surface resources** such as underground water. India has launched remote sensing satellites[2] that help to create maps of underground water to identify locations for drilling wells.

Additionally, international space agencies have put satellites in orbit to track the groundwater disappearing beneath the farmlands of northern India, between Jaipur and Delhi, a stretch of 270 km (170 miles), about the distance between London and Liverpool.

Data from NASA's GRACE Project, collected between 2002-2008, reveals that the **groundwater in Northern India is being used to irrigate crops at a faster rate than the water cycle can replenish the underground aquifers**. The naked eye cannot detect changes in water levels, but twin satellites can measure how much groundwater is withdrawn from the Earth—one foot per year for the last several years.

2. http://www.nasa.gov/topics/earth/features/india_water.html

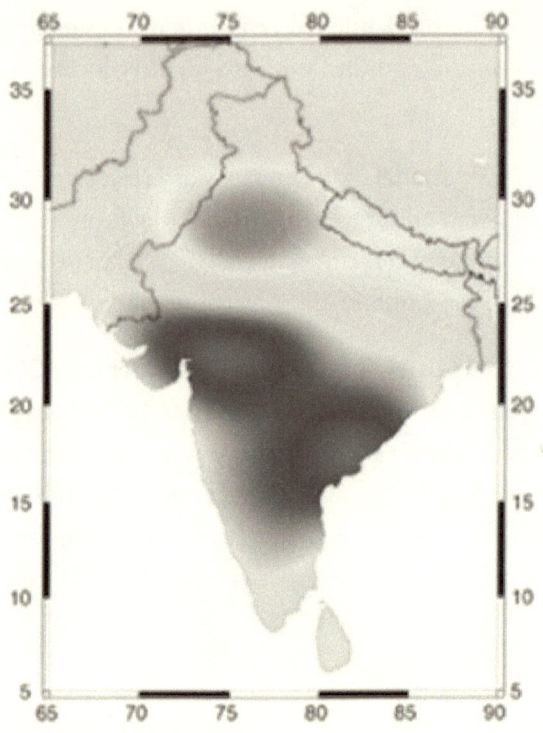

By measuring changes in the gravitational field between the two satellites, changes recorded by a ranging microwave system, and analyzing data recorded by the satellites' instrumentation, **the scientific team can create a _map_ of groundwater gains and losses.** The diagram above shows a *red alert* spot in northern India. By diagnosing the problem, scientists can help the Indian government conserve water—a positive development to be sure!

Satellites *see* and record everything—do they see too much?

Big Brother

Imagine international satellites scanning your phone conversations for *keywords* connected to global terrorism. You may make a joke and say something in all innocence, ignorant of the consequences. Meanwhile, a computer is flagging those words as the satellite transfers the data at lightning speed into a detection-analysis computer program.

Yes, this **keeps us** *safe* from global crime and terrorism. While some think it is necessary, other members of our group have **concerns about their private conversations being monitored** in this way by a sophisticated computer system connected to data-gathering and defense satellites.

And how about cameras in communities such as Glasgow, Scotland, the safest city in the UK, yet the use of **public surveillance cameras is on the rise** (408 cameras compared to 326 in my home city of Paris), what is the purpose? Do surveillance cameras contribute to public safety? How about London, where crime rates have not lowered since the 1980s, yet according to reports, the average citizen in London appears on camera 300 times per day?

We can debate the efficacy of surveillance systems, that's one of those *glass-half-full* or *glass-half-empty* questions, yet as Galacti says, many people worry about their privacy. In contrast, others think, "If you've done nothing wrong, then you have nothing to worry about."

The Space Station, Step to Mars

Space stations are no longer science fiction. The ISS has been host to over 330 men and women from 17 countries since its inauguration in 1998.

How much do we know about space? How much is space contributing to life on Earth? And, how much is humankind doing to maintain the integrity of space around our planet?

We're off to the space station, strapped into a luxury *space tourism* **shuttle** such as Sir Richard Branson's Virgin Galactic or some other spacecraft that might win the X-Prize. While we stare at view-screens which give us images of our journey as well as access to the digital library of the universe, **we think about the actual exploration of space and the discoveries we have made.**

The Kepler Mission, an uncrewed spacecraft, has discovered several new planets in the Kepler-22 star system inside our Milky Way galaxy. The automated Mars Rover *Opportunity* has unearthed discoveries in the 14-mile-wide crater named Endeavour. Japan's Hayabusa spacecraft has visited the asteroid Itokawa to bring back samples.

There are **two private inflatable space modules**, Genesis I and Genesis II, **currently in orbit around the Earth** following their 2006 and 2007 launch, respectively, by the private American firm Bigelow Aerospace.

International Space Station

The international orbital laboratory opens its doors, *so to speak*, and visitors can see the real-life of the ISS—24 hours in space. The front end of the ISS, which houses the space shuttle docking hatch, displays the flags of the fifteen nations involved in creating this monument to international cooperation.

An astronaut aboard the ISS explains **what it is like to begin the day in space**. For example, our audience wants to know: how do you wake up, how do you brush your teeth? The same way you would on Earth, except instead of rinsing out in a sink, the astronaut uses a disposable towel provided by the Russian Space Agency. The astronaut uses a brightly colored cloth to catch the saliva. Afterward, he can even shave inside his small quarters.

Our astronaut wears regular street clothes while aboard the space station and doesn't change them very often, especially since the environment of the space station is more sterile than the streets of wherever the astronauts' home cities happen to be.

Time to start the day and go to work. Our astronaut may update computer equipment much as IT departments would on Earth. Alternatively, our astronaut may **check life support systems** and make sure that the electrolysis, the process by which electricity generated by the station's solar panels splits water into its components to ensure oxygen for the ISS inhabitants to breathe.

Our astronaut may assist scientists from all over the world in **doing research,** such as developing vaccines for MRSA and Salmonella bacteria. Or the astronaut may **participate in a spacewalk** to maintain the Hubble Space Telescope. Russians, Americans, Canadians, all are working in this community, shielded from the vastness and coldness of space.

It is stimulating and inspiring to think that astronauts from different cultures and countries can live and work in the space station, 24/7, in cooperation with each other, in harmony. **On Earth, a multinational effort** from France, Japan, Russia, America, Canada, French Guiana, Germany, the Netherlands, and Italy **supports and maintains the ISS program**.

Given space being so vast and since we haven't achieved the old science-fiction ideals of putting colonies on the Moon, one traveler wants to know whether what we've accomplished is real progress. After all, establishing a settlement on the Moon would be a good testing ground for building one on Mars. What do we know about space?

Side Trip: Dark Matter

I said we weren't going back to the pinhead, but it deserves a brief revisit, as we think of all the matter and energy in the universe—everything in that pinhead—all summed up in a neat little package *The Theory of Everything*.

Scientists now know that there's a substance called **Dark Matter**. Our space shuttle is looking for it, like a kind of *Dark Matter Safari*. We've never observed this, we don't know where it is, in the atmosphere or outer space, but valid calculation, deducted from gravitational effects on visible matter, has evidence that it has to be *there*. **It represents 27% of ALL the matter in the universe,**

Extremely hard to believe, even unimaginable, but it's a fact.

In our dark matter safari, we also seek the substance called **Dark Energy**. Again, it's elusive, like a rare species that never shows itself; however, still realistic computations from the accelerating expansion of the universe show that **it represents 68% of ALL the energy in the universe.**

Again, this is extremely hard to believe, even unimaginable, but it's a fact. The universe, scientists believe, is composed of the two elements Dark Matter at 27% and Dark Energy at 68%[1].

That's 95% of everything in the pinhead at the Big Bang.

One of our passengers examines a test tube containing a *soup* that represents **the remaining 5%**: all the atoms, protons, mesons, baryons, quarks[2] that we can *observe,* albeit not with the naked eye and measure to deduce mathematical equations and theorems. But suppose the visitor reduces that soup to 0.4%, the part of the universe we can actually see. **It's like taking four pieces of a 1000-piece jigsaw puzzle–with so little information, can we figure out what the universe truly is and all the details that make it work?**

"Imagine basing the *Theory of Spaceflight* or *The Theory of a Dolphin* on such scant knowledge," Galacti comments, eliciting laughter. "And yet we have those theories. We almost have a *Theory of Everything* because when computers predicted the weather for this launch, we may have had a bit of difficulty, but the system worked. Or did it?

---

1. https://science.nasa.gov/astrophysics/focus-areas/what-is-dark-energy

2. https://theexplanation.com/on-atoms-protons-neutrons-electrons/

To an extent, within a few hours, we can predict the weather, but even there, we often come up short despite the powerful computers at our disposal. **We are the most advanced and progressive generation scientifically since man walked the Earth, but studying with only 0.4% of the universe visible to the naked eye, we're in for many, many, many surprises."**

Space Debris. Human Pollution

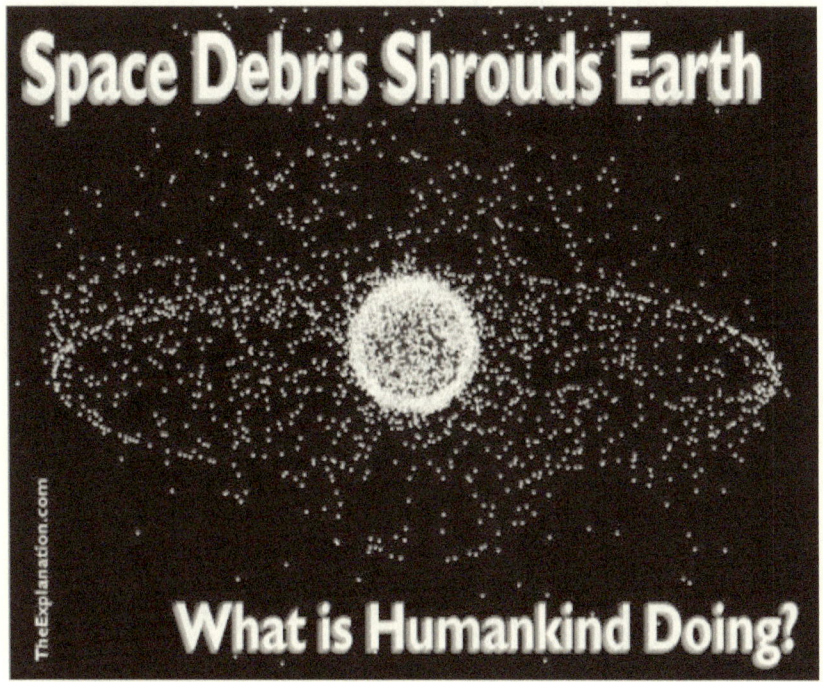

Space, beyond Earth's atmosphere, the vastest, pristine domain—or is it? Space debris is accumulating at an alarming rate.

Space Debris

Down here on Earth, peering up into the vast sky, gazing at the stars, planets, and galaxies makes us **realize just how vast and majestic outer Space is**. However, the naked eye can't see the 1400 km thick sphere enveloping our planet just beyond Earth's atmosphere **where a Formula 1 race of out-of-control space debris, with no pit stops and no rules, whirls around day in day out**.

"Please deposit all trash into the recycle bins," Galacti announces. "**We can't take the chance that microbes from your coffee cups or the crusts of bread from your plate might leak out into Space.** As it is, the International Space Station crew tossed out plastic bags of solid waste, and they had quite a disposal problem when their plumbing broke. They also lost a tool bag while working outside the space station, but they weren't able to track it."

Many objects, including some costly ones, have drifted out of our *view* in Space. Earth's radar dishes have been pointed at orbits around Mercury, for example, where space shuttles have voyaged—but space shuttles and satellites do go missing, as opposed to being in stealth mode (more on that in a moment).

How can a space shuttle just wander away if we have shuttle-tracking radar dishes aimed at the orbits around Mercury? Galacti notes it's not possible to monitor every orbit with radar dishes, and **satellites and spacecraft missions periodically malfunction and go *missing*** before ground crews detect that there is anything wrong. More space debris.

Some of those missions also end up smashed on the Moon, strewn here and there across the flat moonscape. Granted, you can have satellites merrily orbiting the Moon for a century or, as mentioned, sustaining our cell phone signals.

It seems beyond belief that we would *lose* something so complex as a non-reusable Russian space shuttle or a U.S. satellite, which cost, $10,000, and upwards, per pound ($22,000 per kilogram).

Space satellites, stray pieces from the early days of the space shuttle, and even future space missions to explore asteroids threaten to clutter the skies. **Satellite-satellite collisions generate space junk that could circle Earth** and threaten other satellites for the next 10,000 years.

What goes up doesn't necessarily come down—not from Space. Would you believe that there's *a "junkyard" of thousands of pieces of scrap floating around*? So much, so that new launchings and satellite placement have to take into account what's in the vicinity—it's an expensive traffic jam. **Mission planners have to calculate orbits around the poles and the equator carefully,** as the smallest change, for example, a piece of space debris striking a satellite, can alter the orbit or even collide and destroy it.

We are far from the point where the *traffic* in Space resembles the traffic in Jakarta, Indonesia, but it is a concern now and into the future. It's **hard enough to believe we can pollute the enormous amounts of water in the oceans worldwide. Now we have to get our minds around the pollution of the infinitely more vastness of Space around planet Earth.**

We are, incidentally, also **polluting the skies with cell phone signals** that block part of the spectrum of radio wavelengths, astronomers, such as the scientists at the Aricebo Observatory, use to look at the cosmos. We look at our cell phones and wonder what we are doing to the universe. What other clutter are we responsible for, and what are we losing?

Scientific **estimates indicate there are more than 670,000 debris 1–10 cm, and around 29,000 larger pieces of trackable space debris,** that can reach eight-ton defunct satellites, the size of a bus, **speeding around Earth in various orbits.**

These are mainly in Low Earth Orbit (LEO), between altitudes of 160 and 2000 km, where all human-crewed space flights (except trips to the Moon) have taken place. As well as the **Geostationary Earth Orbit (GEO), at 36,000 km where weather and communication satellites hover** above one spot in synchronized rotation with the Earth transmitting information from their focal area.

The image reveals the 5.5mm (0.2 inches) entry hole created on Space Shuttle Endeavour's radiator panel by the impact of unknown space debris.

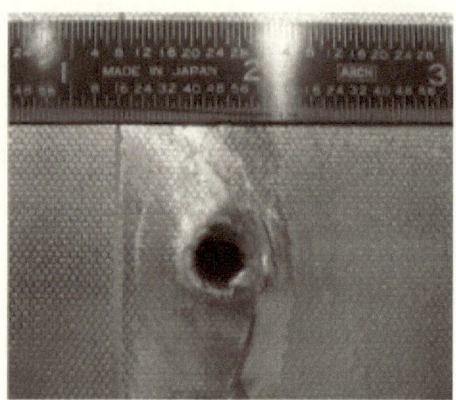

But the **real collision risk comes from an estimated untrackable 170 million debris smaller than 1 cm (0.4 in)**. This flying flotsam is highly dangerous, not only because of its destructive nature, but, as Galacti points out, it may have already reached **critical density**.

This point is when launching and collisions create more space debris—than what is being removed by natural forces like falling out of orbit and being burnt up in the atmosphere; this starts **a chain reaction of pulverizing more and more space debris**.

Small objects such as particles of paint don't leave a significant impact, but, like a piece of gravel cracking your windshield as you drive, they **deteriorate highly polished lenses and solar panels**. Another factor is speed; this space debris is traveling at Mach 9, nine times the speed of sound, and can make shreds out of a satellite. Hypervelocity impacts cause metals to act like fluids, and extreme hypervelocity vaporizes both impactor and target.

We're harnessing the confines of Space for man's necessities, to communicate more and faster, to get better forecasts, and to scrutinize the globe for natural resources. And, in so doing, to what extent are we emptying a full glass? It's been 60 years since we launched our first satellites, humankind has come a long way, technologically. What is the real cost?

The Space Race: Weapons or Manufacturing?

The Space Race isn't which country will win the war, but for humankind's sake, will peaceful, or belligerent pursuits win out?

Manufacturing in Space

It's a space race. We are using Space in unique ways, namely to produce goods necessary for human activity such as top-quality semiconductor chips for computers. Also, protein crystals that can help deliver pharmaceuticals, contact lenses, and aerogels—the lightest solid material known, yet able to support the weight of a compact car—that we use in foam insulation for household windows.

Take the example of contact lenses. Optical manufacturing companies and space agencies have conducted experiments to expose contact lens materials such as fluorine, silicon, and acrylic (fluoro-silicone/acrylate) to the microgravity of Space in pressurized research labs in the Space Shuttle.

The lenses formed under these conditions have proved to be more permeable to gases, thus allowing more oxygen to reach the eyes. Also, these space-manufactured gas-permeable contact lenses are less likely to attract bacteria, preventing eye infections.

Space Wars: Beyond Science Fiction

Our next story, Galacti says, is epic. It concerns **the battle to control the** *ultimate high ground*—**It's the space race.**

A bit of history: **Before June 20, 1944, nothing humanmade had ever entered this** *off-limits* **environment that engulfs Earth.** But World War II and the German V-2 rockets developed by Werner von Braun shattered Space, reaching altitudes up to 200 km, about 100 km into Space. The 'V' stands for Vergeltungswaffe, German for *retaliatory or reprisal weapons* launched against the British.

The story of the weapons space race begins with a personal anecdote for me. My mother described the **German** *terror bombing* **during World War II**, how Londoners could hear the roaring engines of the V-2s arriving over London, and suddenly they'd cease. Moments of anguishing silence as they fell out of the sky, landing, nobody knew where exploding into destruction and indiscriminate death of 7,183 people in England and Belgium.

Paradoxically manufacturing these first space-age weapons took more lives, about 25,000, amongst the forced laborers from the SS concentration camp Dora (Mittelbau KZ)[1]. When Werner von Braun defected to the US, he created a version of **the V-2, which became an inter-mediate-range ballistic missile**. However, the scope of this argument goes beyond the World War II-era conflicts—the story of weapons is much broader.

If we think about armament, we see a progression: hand combat > dagger, sword, spear (pierce, throw, but needs personal contact) > slingshot (trying to hit the enemy from further away) > catapult > gunpowder > guns. Their evolution includes sniper (distance), machine gun (fire-power) > cannon (guns of Navarone and the V-3's which had a range up to 165 km—that's unbelievable). And, even more powerful: atom bomb > missiles > SCUD guided missiles from the Iraq War that fly at ground level following the topography to their target > ICBMs > Missiles from Space. The space race is on.

Galacti brings up a quote:

No superpower has ever decided to become weaker.

The story of **space weapons** also includes **international attempts to restrict or ban them, such as the Outer Space Treaty of 1967**, signed by one hundred nations from Afghanistan to the United States, and the Space Code proposed by the European Union in 2012.

The Outer Space Treaty, designed as a *non-armament* **treaty** based on concerns about the space race even before Russia's launch of Sputnik stipulates, 'an undertaking not to place in orbit around the Earth, install on the moon or any other celestial body, or otherwise station in outer space, nuclear or any other weapons of mass destruction.' It 'limits the use of the moon and other celestial bodies exclusively to peaceful purposes.'

---

1. http://www.v2rocket.com/start/chapters/mittel.html

However, despite international agreements, **the space race has continued between the United States and Russia**, two proponents of the treaty, as well as other players seeking this *ultimate high ground*.

We follow several nations in our story: USA (anti-satellite systems), India (Advanced Air Defence missile interceptor) Russia (anti-missile system), North Korea (UNHA rocket), China (anti-satellite device). There are even joint ventures between nations such as India-Russia (BrahMos cruise missile).

The USA has destroyed a satellite with a missile; China pulverized its own target satellite as well as a medium-range ballistic missile in Space. India is developing a *hit-to-kill* anti-satellite system.

Space is vast, so we think. Why should we worry? International *peace workers* in many countries believe that we have reason to be concerned. Worse, if nations continue to rattle *space sabers* and destroy satellites, we could cripple our world as we know it. Disruption of communication networks and television signals, financial systems wiped out, air traffic controls dismantled, and aircrafts lost—a real disaster scenario.

Space Summary

Space, unlike any other *territory* in our generation, clearly reveals a *before* and *after* status. The intervention of humankind and our effect on Space is visible. We discussed space debris in the last chapter[2].

---

2. http://theexplanation.com/space-debris-humankind-has-managed-to-pollute-earths-space/

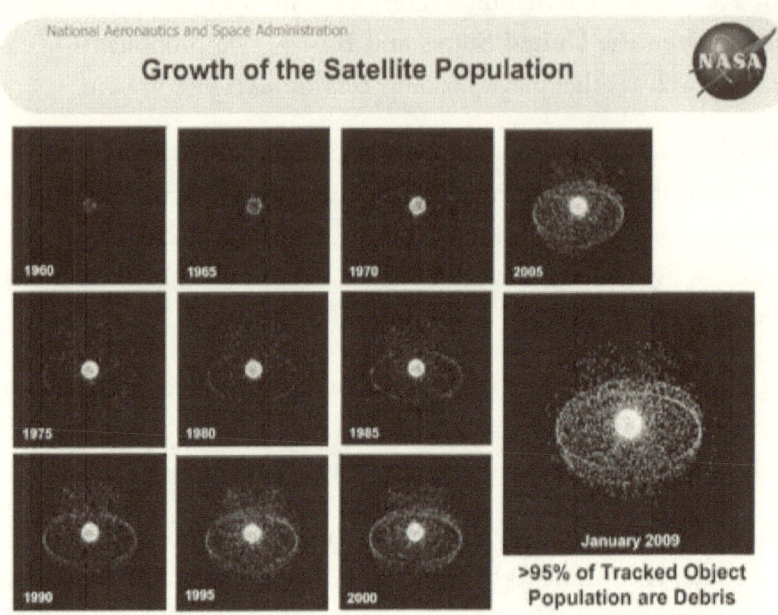

Growth of the Satellite Population

National Aeronautics and Space Administration

>95% of Tracked Object Population are Debris

The above image shows the state of affairs in 1960 (pristine clean) compared with 2009. In just 50 short years, there is an absolute reality of positive and negative.

Space has gone from spotless to soiled, from virgin to adulterated. The unclouded evidence in its transformation should cause humankind to reflect on its behavior.

Have we measured the consequences, the rewards, and penalties? Where will we be in ten or twenty years? Are we making decisions and taking steps to stave off this gnawing situation? Is the glass of peace and prosperity getting fuller or emptier? What is the tendency for humankind?

2. Audit Atmosphere

State of the Earth's Atmosphere

How is Earth's Atmosphere faring nowadays? Is it our breath of life or our wheeze of death?

Via satellites and planes, we explore the atmosphere. In essence, it's part of our daily lives; there is little that we do in which the atmosphere, with the **carbon cycle, nitrogen cycle, oxygen, weather**, and so on, doesn't play a role in some way. Likewise, the bulk of human activity shapes our atmosphere and, by extension, our world. Our atmosphere is the protective envelope of the Earth[1] as we've seen, no other planet, to our knowledge, has such a hospitable background for life.

How, exactly, **is human life changing the atmosphere**, and specifically the Earth's climate, for *good* or *bad*? The stories in this chapter will unfold and "air" all the evidence.

Galacti is once again our tour guide/real estate agent. "I'm afraid Earth is a bit of a *fixer-upper* these days," he says.

---

1. https://theexplanation.com/earths-atmosphere-ingredients-life/

"What happening?" I ask.

"Ah...well, do you see that unobstructed view of Alaska in June, and Beijing all year round?"

"**I can't see Beijing because of smog.** What happened?" I repeat my question.

"Let's start by examining what has happened to the three components of the atmosphere," Galacti says. "In our last tour, it was all about location, location, and location. Now it's climate, climate, and climate!"

From Heart attack to Fertilizer: Nitrogen Impact

Nitrogen is essential for all life. If you are a heart patient taking nitroglycerin pills, you have an excellent idea of how we need nitrogen. People who have high blood pressure and are at high risk for heart attack or angina (chest pain) carry nitroglycerin pills, tablets, patches, tongue spray and ointment with tape for application with them at all times, to take at the first sign of trouble.

It is dispersed in a capsule, so you can't blow anything up with these pills. **What the nitroglycerin does is dilate the blood vessels**, which reduces the blood flow to the heart and creates a drop in blood pressure in the arteries, so that the heart does not pump as hard—less blood and oxygen needed, the heart calms down, the heart relaxes. **Nitrogen, in this case, can save lives.**

"That's the practical application of nitrogen," Galacti says. "On this planet, **you have creative people who think of these things.**"

However, you can have too much of a good thing. In essence, **human activities now remove more nitrogen from the atmosphere than all natural processes combined, and much of this nitrogen ends up as**

a pollutant. A particularly serious problem is nitrate pollution from **agricultural runoff** in ground and surface water supplies, which can poison humans and other living creatures drinking polluted waters.

Nitrates can also significantly **change freshwater and marine ecosystems, creating *dead zones*** (more on this in the next chapter) and poisoning fish. An excess of nitrogen oxides from traffic emissions combines with other pollutants from industry as well as hot weather and forms ozone, a pollutant, and protectant (the proverbial *ozone layer*).

"Here we are at our first stop," Galacti says.

We join scientists at a floating laboratory in the Indian Ocean, in a narrow shipping lane between Sri Lanka and Singapore. We aren't here to contemplate the view of the water, but rather to **consider the orange trails of nitrous oxide or NOx** we see. The scientists are tracking the pathways of nitrous oxide and excess ozone across the globe. But, because of the clarity of the air here, it is easier to see nitrous oxide trails than along the coast of, say, industrialized oil-drilling China or the United States (most of the scientists on this floating laboratory work for NASA).

There are many examples of NOx pollution. Coal-burning factories, agricultural emissions, transportation, and medical factories produce the equivalent weight of 100 Empire State Buildings of NOx gas in the air annually. It is worldwide and specifically in high-emission countries such as the US, China, Brazil, India, and Russia.

There's a recommended limit for exposure to the planet: The Kyoto Protocol recognizes **nitrous oxide in the atmosphere as being 300 times more potent than carbon dioxide.** "In this neighborhood, we have standards—you can't just pollute," Galacti says. "When there's overexposure, especially if we don't have sufficient oxygen in the atmosphere—nitrous oxide destroys the beneficial ozone as well, bringing about change in global temperatures."

Selling Air: Oxygen

As we've seen, our blood carries oxygen[2], once called *fire air*, throughout our bodies and is a crucial ingredient in biological life, in photosynthesis and respiration, in carbohydrates, fats, fatty acids, amino acids, and proteins. **We know that oxygen is essential for life/breath, and also generating energy in cells**, but oxygen deserves praise beyond that.

"Our next stop is an oxygen bar in Vegas, and then on to Beijing," Galacti announces.

Galacti's Sidebar

The world record for a person to hold their breath was set by Stig *Aqauman* Severinsen when he held his breath for 22 minutes. Most of us can handle a few seconds to a minute or so. Under stress, it's even less than that. The composition of the air, the temperature, and the consistency (altitude) impact the amount of time people can hold their breath.

Many **athletes** train at high altitudes to develop their lungpower. **Astronauts** wearing spacesuits and **swimmers** wearing diving suits remind us that **outside our surface environment, hostility waits**, and we must be prepared to navigate these alien regions that are not hospitable to human life.

We humans can't survive without oxygen, and to that end, we spend money on treatments at *oxygen bars*, establishments around the world where we receive oxygen treatments in all different colors. You would

---

2. https://theexplanation.com/blood-and-breath-heart-lungs-maintaining-life-for-80-years/

think we would get more than enough oxygen in our daily lives because we all breathe the same air—however, that's precisely the problem! **Industrialized and not-so-advanced cities are battling the same issues**: Beijing, China, London, England, Ludhiana in India, Ahwaz in Iran, and Ulaanbaatar in Mongolia.

"Welcome to **Beijing**, China," Galacti says. "Home of the Forbidden City. **Please put on your air pollution masks now**. You will notice that in this neighborhood, everyone wears these masks." The city regularly exceeds accepted levels of **fine particles**—less than 2.5 micrometers (PM2.5) in diameter. They are **so small you need an electron microscope to detect them**. They're produced by all types of combustion like motor vehicles, coal-burning, and other power plants, residential wood burning, agricultural burning, forest fires, and many other industrial processes.

In response to warnings from the World Health Organization that the air in Beijing and Northern China has exceeded international air quality standards, a **Chinese multimillionaire is selling oxygen in colorful _soft drink_ aluminum cans**.

"Wow, that sounds as if he is taking advantage of the situation," Galacti comments. "On the other hand, I've heard he wants to draw attention to what you humans are doing to the air. Can of air, anyone? You'll need it to live in Beijing. We can make a deal..."

The measurements in Beijing[3] can be as disturbing as the **London Fog**, also dubbed the _Great Smog_ of 1952 in which 4,000 people died—mainly elderly and young people, as well as those with respiratory and heart ailments, with 8,000 more deaths in the weeks following the miasma.

---

3. http://aqicn.org/city/beijing/

It was a *perfect storm* of exceptionally high coal-burning byproducts. **Particulate matter** of smoke, sulfur dioxide, sulphuric acid, fluorine compounds, and hydrochloric acids **was 56 times normal levels** for the period, All these known industrial pollutants, combined with near-zero temperatures, high pressure, and mild winds, trapped the smog in the city for several days.

How certain can we be that pollution was the cause of squeezing out the oxygen? In 1956 Britain passed the Clean Air Act that established *smokeless zones*. Other legislation followed to prevent such a dire situation from occurring again. The smog was so bad that **the environmental movement was born.**

Sadly, London today is still smog-filled, and 4,000 people die yearly from harmful pollutants.

"You'll **notice a thick nasty haze blocking the plains of Northern China** (as well as London), so what the Chinese billionaire is doing to sound the alarm about the problem is a noble goal," Galacti says. "But if you're looking for clean air, let's do some more searching and see if we find some. **Where does all the pollution come from?"** Is the *can* half-empty or half-full?

Carbon Dioxide Worldwide

Carbon dioxide levels in the atmosphere are increasing. Do we want polluted cities and tropical rain forests? Or fresh air, vibrant forests, and livable cities?

Carbon Dioxide and the Greenhouse Effect

As we have seen in examining the burning of stars[1] and in viewing pre-historic Earth, **carbon** is the fourth most abundant element in the universe. It is part of the atmosphere, inanimate objects (diamonds) and all living organisms, and **makes life possible**, *better living through organic chemistry*. In its purest form, carbon is non-toxic to humans and animals.

---

1. https://theexplanation.com/star-formation-how-is-it-possible/

Climate change, based on human activity such as burning fossil fuels, agricultural **development, and reckless industrialization**, within the last two centuries, is real. Methane, nitrogen oxides, and carbon dioxide are the *harvest* we reap from this activity. **The end products are air contamination, ozone belt destruction, and acid rains, as well as an excess of carbon dioxide.** We see a steady rise of 316 parts per million (ppm) in the air in 1958 to 400 ppm in 2013, an increase of 27 percent in 55 years.

Stations in Alaska, Greenland, Hawaii, Britain, Russia, India record 400 ppm. **The safe amount of CO_2 is 350 ppm** according to global consensus. **What is 400 ppm, and what does it mean?** Except for the prehistoric and pre-Homo Sapiens era, until the recent period between 1958-2013, the concentrations of CO_2 were at 280 in the industrial period—350 is the safe limit. **400 may be the difference between record temperatures, the Canadian Arctic being completely green** (as it was 2.5 million years ago during parts of the Ice Age), and having glaciers worldwide. However, we are hitting 400 again within a short span, even if it is just a moment in geologic time.

Tropical forests are razed to make way for pastures where cattle can graze and for buying tropical wood products such as furniture made from mahogany and African okoumé. Even pencils and toilet plungers that contain rainforest wood contribute to the lack of oxygen-producing trees.

See this video, New York city's green gas emissions[2].

The gases given off by burning fossil fuels allow the atmosphere to retain more infrared heat rays that warm or *microwave* the Earth gradually. **Today the CO_2 concentrations are off-the-charts higher than at any period in the past three million years.**

---

2. https://youtu.be/DtqSIplGXOA

CO2: West Antarctic Ice Sheet, Greenland, Alaska

Glaciers all over the world are shrinking, from the Perto Moreno Glacier in Argentina to the Tibetan Glacier, from the Glacier National Park in Montana to the most prominent ice shelf in the Arctic, the Wharton Ice Shelf that cracked in half in 2003. The most striking example is the West Antarctic Ice Sheet (WAIS).

"Take a look at that beautiful sheet of ice, folks. Historic and pristine," Galacti says. "Unfortunately, it's also cracking. It's disintegrating. Definitely signs of wear and tear as we like to say in the real estate biz."

A team of scientists and activists travel underneath the polar ice shelf in a nuclear submarine, wanting to see the disintegration of these majestic glaciers up close.

Land-based ice has crumbled at rapid rates, cascading like a tower of cards. The loss of ice in the stunning, pristine West Antarctic sheet is measurable: a 40 percent reduction in 40 years. Our team of scientists has mapped 54 ice shelves around Antarctica and discovered twenty of them that are melting because of predominantly West Antarctic warm ocean currents.

When we debate *climate change* and whether it is occurring, whether the world is warming, we can talk about cooling temperatures as some have, but **the shrinking of the West Antarctic Ice Sheet is a fact**. We have all the data from the main ice cores (cylinders of ice nearly half a foot in diameter collected from the depths of the ice sheet) to show the history of carbon dioxide. Four hundred thirty thousand years worth of data—to put this in perspective, 430,000 years ago, beings were first learning to make pigments by hand.

What does CO_2 have to do with the WAIS, dubbed the most unstable glacier in the world? Some people argue that changes in the WAIS don't amount to much as evidence of humans affecting climate or **anthropogenic climate change**. It increases heat in the ice and deepwater that is directly linked to the steady increase in CO_2 shown by the ice cores. It is causation, not correlation.

Physics and the very act of measuring the ice cores and calculating the human-made CO_2, which is double the average atmospheric CO_2, are objective, real ways of determining what we know: that increased levels of carbon dioxide also increase the optimum temperature of the Earth's surface.

OK, we get it, we know that CO_2 plays a role in what we are seeing. **What exactly does the West Antarctic Ice Sheet do for the world?** To put it another way: Why should we travelers and readers of *The Explanation* care? Is it essential to have vast sheets of ice, and not just for aesthetic reasons? Is this truly a world problem? Aren't glaciers somewhat smaller and less numerous than in the past?

The West Antarctic Ice Sheet is the vastest single mass of ice on Earth and is the only remaining ice sheet from the last glacial period that ended 12,500 years ago. Its impact is much more than that, as we will see when we examine the state of water in the world in the next chapter of *Audit of the Universe*.

The melting of 98 percent of Greenland's surface ice is possibly explained by a change in the jet stream that trapped warmer high-pressure systems over colder areas. Greenhouse gas levels in Alaska and Greenland, as everywhere, have registered at 400 ppm

Do we need glaciers, or are warm days in June in Alaska or a hotter summer at the WAIS a severe problem? The short answer is that **ice sheets act as reflectors of the sun's heat away from Earth**. They are, in effect, a **vital part of Earth's temperature control system**. The more ice sheets you have, the more reflection you get with a resultant lower overall atmospheric temperature.

The counterpart is **the fewer ice sheets you have, the more the heat is absorbed both by the water and the land exposed by the disappearing ice sheets**. This extra heat accelerates the melting of the ice sheets, causing the irreversible conditions that scientists now refer to as **the point of no return**. See this video about the Melting of Antarctica[3].

3. https://assets.ngeo.com/modules-video/latest/assets/ngsEmbedded-
Video.html?guid=0000015c-d03a-d1cb-a7fd-d4ff0b610000

Climate Change: Reality or Fiction?

Climate Change is a daily subject nowadays—not to say a controversial one. Billions of people and Billions of Dollars are at stake. What do you think?

Climate change, atmospheric conditions, weather upsets, temperature fluctuations, whatever we want to call it, it makes daily headline news around the world. Televisions and Radio weather forecasts refer to topsy-turvy meteorology, which has become a buzzword in the last few years. Whether we like it or not, it's part of our audit of the atmosphere.

Heat Waves

In 2003, in my home city of Paris, we experienced **record temper-atures** at the same time as the rest of Europe, and the temperatures caused 70,000 deaths across the continent, in the UK, Italy, Spain, the Netherlands, and Portugal for example, with 15,000 deaths in France alone. Many cities were unprepared for the minimum 40 degrees Celsius (104 degrees Fahrenheit) temperatures.

Paris has cool nights year-round, and certainly not used to the wildfires that raged through France. The historic architecture of Paris mixed with the concrete of the city created a *heat sink* or heat island from which there was no relief, especially for the elderly. The hospitals were full.

French authorities were concerned about **nuclear meltdowns** since the high temperatures made cooling the 58 reactors (in 2003) difficult. Nuclear plants have a 50° Celsius or 122° Fahrenheit threshold. In the heat, the plants expel cooling liquid more rapidly than usual, making the reactors hotter. In the 40 degrees Celsius environment, conditions in the plants spurred the French to spray nuclear cores with water.

The conditions were no better elsewhere in Europe. There were forest fires in Portugal, flash floods from melting glaciers in the Swiss Alps, 9,000 older people dead in Germany. The 2003 heat disaster in Europe was the **first time we could explicitly link mass death and suffering to global warming and climate change**—a sobering example, to be sure. Europe has never dealt with such extreme temperatures.

Imagine burning orchards in Portugal, where **firefighters admitted to being completely overwhelmed by the blazes**. Tiny sun-drenched is-lands in the Adriatic Sea have gone up in flames. Irrigation ditches and water wells dry from the heat in Italy. In Switzerland, the ancient per-mafrost melts, causing avalanches. Europe feels fire hazards and the ice crunch.

The year 2013 was cold, and there were vast amounts of rain and erratic weather in the UK. There was flooding in the US. **In the UK, this extreme weather links to the Arctic sea ice loss.** According to a team of US and UK scientists that study the changing temperature and pressure gradients, there's a connection with the melting sea ice.

Climate—associated with atmospheric conditions—has become a much-used word in the last few years, unfortunately in a more foreboding way. That's why *The Explanation* asks the question, is the glass of peace and prosperity getting fuller or emptier when it comes to living conditions on Earth?

Fleeing Climate Change

Climate change[1], temperature change that is going on now, is not just a remote issue; it is affecting where people live and work, their very livelihoods and existence.

"Welcome to the **Maldives**, a tiny island nation you never think about—**the president of that country is considering resettling his people in other countries**, and is *house-hunting* internationally because of rising ocean levels and increased pollution." The highest island is in the Addu Atoll, it's 2.4 m (yes, just a little more than the tallest basketball player, Paul Sturgess at 2.34 m) and the Atoll is home to over 32.000 people.

Galacti says. "These small island nations are tropical, poetic, romantic, and vulnerable, folks. Fifty small island nations such as the **Maldives could fully disappear in twenty to thirty years**. Imagine whole islands where populations have lived a precarious existence for centuries, suddenly vanishing from the face of the Earth. Even people who still have

---

1. https://theexplanation.com/earths-atmosphere-ingredients-life/

a nation are forced to flee in search of safety, security, and family. Look at these people; they won't give you a good review of their part of this property."

We can see this in the face of a woman in **Bangladesh or India or Indonesia or even New Orleans** post-Hurricane Katrina, a woman affected by the global sweep of a cyclone that makes landfall. Rising ocean temperatures in the Atlantic Ocean and the Gulf of Mexico, in the Indian Ocean, mean increased storms: As the water temperature increases, the wind velocity of a storm passing over the Indian Ocean increases.

In the direct path of the flood and storm, the woman we have just met grabs her children and flees her home, a wooden homestead with a blue-tiled roof or perhaps a modern American home. Now, living in a refugee shack near the railroad in Dhaka, Bangladesh, or in a FEMA trailer in New Orleans or even temporarily in the Superdome in Texas.

Families struggle to remain calm, recalling their experience, as do people in the Yup'ik Eskimo village of 350 inhabitants, Newtok, **Alaska, where massive flooding threatens to displace people from their ancestral homes.** It's the same region where the aerial photo of an unusually bright Alaska is taken, and Newtok itself is completely clear. (Scientists estimate that 180 Native Alaskan villages are vulnerable.) The state has warmed twice as fast as the rest of North America within the timespan of 1958-2013.

Unfortunately, situations where climate change comes directly into play, are more and more frequent. What about the planetary response?

Extreme Events

Extreme weather is not a reality yet; however, there are *black swan* or **unexpected events linked to climate change.** A team of climatologists uses the satellite data we gathered on the weather, as well as past data on bizarre meteorology patterns, to create a *global hotspot* map for the weather. The scientists use *pop-ups* at each location—mini-movies that tell stories, such as the older people in the 2003 European heatwave. **Other stories that have a medium to high correlation with climate change:**

- Wales/UK, 2000 and 2007: Villagers on the coast of Wales endure the wettest summer and autumn on record since 1766. The coastlines erode. Villages in peril.
- Eastern Mediterranean/Middle East, 2008: All across Italy, Croatia, Turkey, Iran, Iraq, Syria, etc., farmers suffer through the driest winter since 1902. Winter/spring wheat and cereals are damaged. The farmers struggle to produce enough for their livelihoods and their families.
- Victoria, Australia, 2009: Devastating heatwave that sparks wildfires and destroys 3,500 homes, killing several families. The province weeps as 173 people die.
- Western Russia, 2010: Hottest summer recorded since 1500. Wildfires destroy 25 percent of crops around Moscow, as well as several homes. Heat and wildfires kill 55,000 people, including Muscovites and farmers.
- Continental US, 2012: Following the four-state wildfire blaze of 2011, the US experiences severe crop-killing drought caused by the warmest July since 1895. Global food prices skyrocket.

The point is not to be negative but to place facts before us. It has got nothing to do with doomsday or predictions of disaster. *The Explanation* is pursuing an audit of the atmosphere; we're **evaluating the pros and cons of what weather forecasters and climatologists were telling us in 2017.**

Detecting Air Pollution and its Results

Air Pollution is a reality, both invisible and visible. Worldwide, we live with it daily; it's an unwanted guest in our lungs and bodies. The air around us directly affects our health.

Global Health Risks

"If the air pollution, storms, floods, and wildfires don't captivate your attention, then disease might," Galacti says. "Under real estate law, I am required to disclose all health hazards on the property, our planet Earth, which is what I have been doing. We're in the **Sahel in Africa.** where this semi-arid belt of land hasn't always had positive inspections, and where suffering is a daily concern, but it is their home."

Imagine years with no rain in the Sahel or the sub-Saharan part of Africa. As well as East Africa where drought has been trending since the 1970s with diminishing rainfall over the last 20 years. It is of great concern as it affects pastures to maize and, ultimately, the impoverished populations of those regions. **This drought is not just in sub-Saharan Africa; it's** in Russia, where there were dry spells in 2010, 2012 and 2014. Beginning in 2015, although there was a minor improvement in water supply conditions, the British Isles showed some drought intensification.

In Asia, dry conditions continue to focus around Mongolia and northern India. And, in Australia, drought conditions remained relatively constant with some escalation in the interior of the continent. Fire danger is still at a high across New Zealand, where water storage is an on-going issue, particularly on the South Island, where drought had been declared but saw improvement in 2017.

Several women living in a camp or village in the Sahel are concerned with the **stresses of lack of water**[1] in their own country and region. International aid officials on-site share the women's concerns since the drought links to meningitis epidemics as well as outbreaks of diarrhea in Sub-Saharan Africa.

What connection does drought have with disease? **Outbreaks of meningitis** happen more quickly in dry weather because dusty, windy conditions are more prone to invasion, carriage, and transmission of the bacteria coupled with outbreaks of respiratory infections. As for **diarrhea**, unlike mosquitoes, flies multiply faster in drought conditions and transmit the illness-causing bacteria, especially in countries with **poor sanitation** management where *pit toilets* are left uncovered.

"Poor plumbing is a big issue," Galacti comments. "So are the flies."

---

1. https://theexplanation.com/water-resources-coral-reefs-sodas-colorado-river-and-crops/

Other diseases have found a breeding ground because of climate change. For example, in Europe in 2003, **extreme heat** caused circulatory diseases and aggravated respiratory ailments, to which children and the elderly are susceptible. Another effect of heat increase is air pollution from pollens and industrial pollutants. On the surface, the African woman and the elderly grand-mere in Paris have nothing in common, except the weather. **Epidemiologists and climatologists apply their minds to discerning patterns in disease associated with weather conditions.**

On the ground, Les Medecins sans Frontiers, the WHO, or the Red Cross, treat **patients in international clinics** and refugee camps. **A parade of diseases passes through**: tropical illnesses such as dengue fever, Lyme disease, tick-borne encephalitis, Mediterranean spotted fever, diarrhea—human suffering that scientists believe links to weather changes.

For example, in areas with record rainfall and flooding, malaria spreads faster because mosquitoes breed more. **Lyme disease is rising** in areas such as the northern US, as the extension of hotter weather prolongs the active season for disease-carrying ticks that also spread encephalitis and Mediterranean spotted fever. The global health risks are real in this *Earth property*.

Fortunately, practical solutions are being proposed.

Clean Cookstoves, Clean Air, Carbon in the Soil

A woman in Northern Kenya cooks a traditional meal on a squat **open-air cookstove**, the size of a snare drum, made from scrap metal, with a ceramic lining on the inside. The genius of the stove is that it works like a large-scale version of a simple match. An international alliance has made this possible. As you enjoy this traditional meal prepared for you and our group, you are tasting **a potential solution to the problem of climate change**.

For three billion people (mainly women) worldwide, **preparing meals with traditional rudimentary cookstoves is a way of life** that is contributing to climate change and health issues, as well as 3.5 million deaths a year from toxic fumes. As our *clean cookstove*[2] chef finishes cooking without clouds of poisonous smoke, the woman's neighbor coughs from the fumes of burning charcoal as she uses an *old-model* traditional metal stove. Lung cancer has killed several of the women in the family in the *old-model* stove household, as well as children under five years old.

The smoke is also harmful to the atmosphere. Particularly since, in stoves that use wood and coal for fuel, people must either use up all the available timber or clear forests for coal mining operations—fewer plants mean more carbon emissions remain in the air. It is a cycle that keeps repeating because of poverty and **stoves that use resources inefficiently and produce *black carbon*,** which contributes to global warming.

The woman with the *clean cookstove* empties the ceramic drum, **spilling out the remnants of the plant-based fuel it burns. The white-gray fuel, *biochar*, contains nutrients for the soil**, and the woman, as well as her community, will add the biochar to the fields to promote crop growth. "Clean cookstoves seems to be a step in the right direction," says Galacti, "but there are pros and cons in man-made solutions."

Detecting Air Pollution

2. *http://news.nationalgeographic.com/news/energy/2011/02/110215-cookstoves-sustainable-development-ghana/*

The satellites we examined in the last chapter allow us to monitor **air pollution to ensure the health and safety of humans and animals**.

"Any of you that have children listen up. You have asked me about whether this place is family-friendly," Galacti says. "Unfortunately, toxic pollution is harming your babies—it's like secondhand smoke taken to new levels. It's hard to cleanse a house of the smell of tobacco, especially when people continue to smoke."

Researchers worldwide have collaborated in the most extensive study ever conducted that shows pregnant women's exposure to air pollution, emitted by vehicles and coal-burning plants, causes babies to be born with low birth weight. Through a review of data collected over fifty years, scientists determined that **air pollution particles, as thick as soft downy baby hair, are affecting mothers**. The study also noted that nations with tighter restrictions on air pollution, such as European nations, Canada, the US, have lower levels of pollution particles.

Using international satellites, researchers have measured air quality in Europe and the UK, North America, South America, Asia, and Australia. At the same time, they've **correlated data from three million pregnant women in fourteen sites on five continents**: and health risks in large geographic areas and over extended periods. These researchers are skilled at accurately *diagnosing* the pollution from, for example, sulfates released by coal in rural areas.

The team has discovered that **the higher the pollution rate was at the study site, the more likely the women were to have underweight newborns**, weighing less than 2.5 kg or 5.5 pounds. These findings confirm a Harvard study that suggests industrial sources tend to affect newborns more strongly than emissions from automobiles. However, vehicular emissions are still of concern. Consider India, one of the leading sites of the survey, where one in four babies out of the 2.6 million born every year is underweight.

"The hospitals in this part of the property, India, are overwhelmed," Galacti comments. "They're used to seeing underweight babies because of hunger, but **all this pollution is making it worse.**"

Think of a skinny, delicate baby that weighs less than a kilo, born in a Chennai hospital, while three other babies close to him in the same ward look typically healthy. From 2008-2012 Chennai has seen a dramatic increase of underweight babies born (11.7 percent to 15.6 percent in just four years). Lifestyle changes, hypertension, diabetes, and other factors may also contribute, but air pollution from vehicles, burning garbage, factories, etc. all leave airborne particles.

However, environmental research centers (Yale, Columbia) have ranked India last in air quality—pollution levels are five times above the safe limit for humans. **India is the leading country in underweight kids**, not all due to air pollution but primarily due to hunger—in a country that already has child health risks, pollution is a new hazard. Think of a baby struggling to survive, a baby that fits into the palm of one hand—most people would be affected by such a heartbreaking sight.

What does this mean for the underweight babies? They suffer many health problems, delayed mental and physical development, lower immunity to disease from viruses and bacteria, hyperactivity, colic, and so on. They are more likely to die earlier; indeed, low birth weight is one of the leading causes of infant mortality worldwide.

We may not all live in severely polluted countries, but whether we are aware of it or not, **pollution is everywhere**, invisible, or visible. Most of us have become used to microscopic pollutants in our air, in cities, countryside and homes. In the case of Beijing, one of the study centers, the dwellers of certain quarters of that city live with a concentration of particles over 700 micrograms per cubic meter. That's more than

50 times the legal limit in the US and Europe—although China is not yet in India's league in terms of poor-quality air, the Chinese are concerned—the world is watching.

"Pollution affects every square foot of this property," Galacti says. "People are starting to *wake up* to reality."

Gas Emissions: Can we Change?

Environmental Efforts

GOAL	GOAL DESCRIPTION	% MET
	SAN JOSE'S PROGRESS TOWARD 2022 GREEN VISION GOALS	
1	Create 25,000 clean-tech jobs as the world center of clean innovation	40.7%
2	Reduce per capita energy use by 50%	12.6%
3	Receive 100% of electrical power from clean, renewable sources	21%
4	Build or retrofit 50 million square feet of green buildings	13.4%
5	Divert 100% of waste from landfill and convert waste to energy	73%
6	Recycle or beneficially reuse 100% of our wastewater	26.5%
7	Adopt a general plan with measurable standards for sustainable development	61.1%
8	Ensure 100 percent of public fleet vehicles run on alternative fuels	40%
9	Plant 100,000 new trees; replace all streetlights with smart, zero-emission lighting	8.6%; 4%
10	Create 100 miles of trails connecting with 400 miles of on-street bikeways	54.75%

Will they Pay Off?

TheExplanation.com

Gas Emissions are the key to clean atmospheric conditions. Is the worldwide gauge heading towards a more murky or radiant environment?

Al Gore

A *property expert* on Earth, former United States Vice-President **Al Gore Jr.**, weighs in on the state of real estate. "Imagine," Galacti says, "he was the one who said, the *most vulnerable part of the Earth is the atmosphere*! He **organized the first hearings on global warming** in the United States in the 1970s, but his focus has been on the entire Earth and the climate."

Al Gore has traveled the world, visiting many of the same places and seeing the same phenomena detailed in the stories we've shared thus far in this book, observing and reporting the same stunning effects of atmospheric change. **He called Hurricane Sandy, in 2012, a warning.** As the bizarre storm approached the Eastern US, according to Gore, the hurricane's storm surge gained strength and power from aberrantly warm coastal waters as well as sea-level rise.

On his tour, Al Gore **speaks to an audience in China,** talking about how we have filled the atmosphere, of the *picture-perfect* Earth from space, with pollution. A Chinese-English banner honors the lecture he is giving. Just hours before, he has been in planes, in cars, writing the story of the *call to action* he is making now.

He speaks of walls of water destroying property in Katrina—crops destroyed by extreme heat—a hurricane in Honduras in 1998 that left 1.5 million people homeless—events that he literally and metaphorically ties to his maps and bar graphs. He can cite figures on CO_2 gas emissions and Alaska's ice retreating. But what reaches millions of people worldwide is the stories Al Gore tells of **how what humans are doing to the atmosphere affects all corners of the globe.** It impacts all humans in various circumstances, regardless of race, region, religion, or wealth.

Cool Cities: San Jose, California

In our last story, Al Gore has pointed to the **need for individuals to create solutions**—can one person make a difference? How about one city, or a network of cities? Since we've established that one location does indeed affect the atmosphere for the world—in ways we don't realize—let's focus on one city, a corner of our *property*.

In the US and Canada, the City of San Jose joins such cities as Ottawa, Canada, Elmhurst, Illinois, and Lansing, Michigan, in signing on for a series of milestones to bring about real change for the better. After taking the first step in signing the US **Mayors Climate Protection Agreement** (Canada has a similar one), San Jose passed a law for a reduction of 25% of greenhouse gas emissions. The city aims to nearly quadruple the reduction to 80 percent below 1990 levels by 2045. San Jose made progress in meeting its 2012 goal. Unfortunately, the next 4-year plan took a dip. Hopefully, they can turn it around.

With its **10-point Green Vision Plan, the City Council is providing leadership for the Sierra Club Cool Cities San Jose team**, which unites organizations and small groups of citizens in the effort to reduce greenhouse gas emissions citywide. Part of this effort is to educate individuals, organizations, and businesses about the benefits of reducing greenhouse gas emissions and energy efficiency.

"One point of the Green Vision Plan we like: Ensure that **100 percent of public fleet vehicles run on alternative fuels**," Galacti says. "Also: **Divert 100 percent of the waste in the landfill** and convert 100 percent of the waste to energy." Practical steps towards *home improvement*, but do they work? As for the first, since 2007, 40 percent of the public vehicles (buses, police cars, etc.) now run on alternative fuel.

San Jose built mass transit and high-speed rails, expanded the city's network of charging stations. Forty percent of cars switched to clean natural gas, bio-diesel, bi-fuel/clean natural gas unleaded blend, electric, electric-unleaded hybrid, and other *green* energies such as methane. **In so doing, the city has been able to reduce consumption of fuel and greenhouse gas emissions** from 1,307,191 gallons and 18,232 tons, respectively, to 982,003 gallons and near the target of 13,000 tons.

Concerning the fuel, imagine one person in the city fleet driving the equivalent of 65,000 miles or a car in need of serious maintenance per year, cutting back on the commute and driving 40,000 miles—still a great deal of driving. Yet, the **vehicle is in better shape, and there are reduced gas emissions.** The 18,000 tons of emissions, the equivalent of toxic metals in noxious coal ash waste, is being reduced to nearly 13,000 tons, or the equivalent of harmful volcanic debris that covered the airport in Yakima, Washington, following the Mt. St. Helens eruption of 1980.

As for the second, **the city conducts *waste phaseout* sessions**, and 73 percent of trash has been diverted and, through city partnerships with corporations, converted to *green energy* such as biodiesel, biogas, and so on.

San Jose sends 494,000 tons of garbage to landfills annually, and in the six years since enacting the plan, reduced that to just 133,380 tons. Multiply that by six, and that's 800,280 tons as opposed to 2.9 million—imagine several open cargo containers, all stinking up the air until it is unbearable. **Reduced by nearly three-quarters—the stench does not go away but is more bearable.**

What can one city or even a network of cities do? **Consider the *eco-cities*,** communities either founded on or adapted to self-sufficient, self-sustaining industry and energy, of Freiberg, Germany, Auroville, India, Curitiba, Brazil, and Stockholm, Sweden, recognized as *The European Green Capital* in 2010. **Although the challenges of developing *eco-cities* are great and difficult to achieve, select communities are accomplishing much.**

Carbon Tax

"Living on this planet entails some cost to improve and upgrade," Galacti says. "Some humans want to have a *special assessment*, the way many of you do in your towns and cities, neighborhoods, and home-owner's associations." This *particular assessment* is called the carbon tax, and many people feel that it is too much to pay and would take money and resources away from other *improvements*. **The carbon tax is designed to make people change their habits** and drive more emission-efficient cars, use fewer luxury goods that consume energy, and so on.

In **China**, which we've covered in detail, there is a proposed carbon tax of 10 yuan per tonne of carbon dioxide, increased to 50 yuan by 2020, a jump from $1.60 to $4.40. Most of this tax will be applied to **coal** and will chiefly affect exports of Chinese goods, resulting in higher prices that may not be affordable worldwide. In **Australia**, the price is $23 per tonne and has upset the 10,000 coal miners that have lost jobs—the carbon tax proved to be a tough sell for Australia's former prime minister. **Emissions have dropped by 7 percent** from 2011 to the present, a figure that could be due to decreased demand and installing solar panels.

In **2020 in the UK**, the price of carbon could rise to 54 Euros per tonne, which UK businesses say will cost them 9.3 billion pounds, which they will pass on to the consumer. **Yes, it can curb gas emissions** as we see in Australia, but **can businesses afford it?** Subsidies for bio-fuels have reduced the price of gasoline, encouraging people to drive more, thus possibly increasing emissions—we mention this to point out **a solution that was supposed to be good but is making the climate worse.**

Man can be his own worst enemy even in trying to solve problems—despite some gains and improved environment, is the economic hardship of the *carbon tax* worth it?

Conclusion

We have *airspace,* but **the air is there for everyone**—China, America, Africa, Russia, Europe, the Middle East, Oceania. Our international tour group forms a significant world convention and **ponders the state of the air**. We take a moment just to breathe—smog-filled air, pure air, oxygen tanks—we need all the oxygen we can get because next, we are going to be diving into deep waters.

3. Audit Water

The Hydrologic Cycle has Changed

The hydrologic cycle continues unabated, but drying up and removing wetlands forces water to run off and accumulate where it wouldn't usually go.

Water tells the story of humankind and Earth. First, we are composed of water. Second, water shapes land both by years of erosion and by depositing sand, sediment, and salt in the shape of basins and river deltas and alluvial fans, which form deserts. Third, you can trace the migration of humankind throughout the world back to the rivers, seas, lakes, and oceans.

We are at the Water Cycle Café[1], which to recap *Inventory of the Universe*, is a European or American-style diner restaurant that looks like the entire Earth, where air, water, and food interrelate and ordering, cooking, serving and disposal run on the hydrologic cycle: precipitation > canopy interception > snowmelt > runoff > infiltration > subsurface (groundwater) flow > evaporation > condensation > sublimation (absorption).

This time, however, the Café is closed. How can that be? The water cycle[2] never stops, does it?

We have never thought about the history of water in human civilization, in agriculture and industry, of **humans as stewards of water. Yet,** we are, and we have been for centuries.

Is the Water Café still viable?

How much of the freshwater in the world is accessible for drinking, bathing, washing, and all vital human activities? In other words, who has access to water? Would you believe that **11 percent of humanity, or 783 million people, has no access to clean drinking water?**

Galacti, dressed in a waiter's uniform, wonders, "There are finite, limited quantities of fresh water on the world menu. What are you humans doing with it?"

---

1. https://theexplanation.com/water-cycle-brushing-your-teeth-flushing-toilet/

2. https://theexplanation.com/water-cycle-brushing-your-teeth-flushing-toilet/

Consider that in **Bangladesh, it alternates between drought**, with dams in India keeping water away from Bangladesh during the dry season, **and rain**. The country can be 70 percent underwater, imagine women washing and doing chores in waist-deep water. The Gorai River in Bangladesh/India is changing course in the dry season and drying up, so much that in a few more years, it will be permanently cut off from the Ganges, leaving many without water.

We view a protest by Bangladesh and Indian citizens who are fighting the construction of dams in India. We have never thought about **protests over a river** a world away for most of us. **Human activities shape the environment**, and the hydrologic cycle, sometimes in dramatic and deliberate ways with unintended consequences.

Nile River/Aswan Dam

In the Water Cycle Café, a dam blocks the natural flow of the water. We meet an **Egyptian official and an Ethiopian farmer.** The farmer believes she and her people have a right to their share of the resources of the Nile, and she has **petitioned her government to divert more of the Nile River.** Thanks to a project named the Renaissance Dam, she'll have more water for her fields and her neighbors' fields, and more energy for her country.

"We have water for teff grass, the staple of Ethiopia that is used to make spongy injera bread, and energy, not necessarily for the people of Egypt," Galacti announces. "That's the blue plate special, 1,300 to 6,600 billion gallons of water going to Ethiopia and flowing out of Egypt—which gets the majority of the water since 1956."

The **Egyptian official strongly protests the move**, aided in his protests by international agencies, and an official from **Sudan rejects any Ethiopian claim to a more significant share of the water.**

Meanwhile, the global crusader Wikileaks reveals plans that the **Egyptian and Sudanese governments have drawn up for a launching pad that will enable an attack by Egypt against the Ethiopian Grand Renaissance Dam.** It, along with the other dams in Ethiopia, generate 4,612 MW of electricity, over double the Hoover Dam, which supplies a good part of California, Nevada, and Arizona.

Unlike coal-fired plants, there are **few drawbacks to hydroelectric power**—except, of course, in this case where there is armed conflict over water as a resource. The Egyptian and Sudanese officials must face the ire of the Ethiopian farmer and her neighbors, with whom they plead to support a new leader in Ethiopia who can resolve the conflict.

The farmer in Ethiopia is tired of having to scratch out a living in drought conditions. At the same time, the Egyptians enjoy the lush Nile River valley and the benefits the water brings (although the Nile is far from pristine). The Egyptians argue that they invented hydroelectric power and should have dams, although, in the region, **Ethiopia is now ahead of Egypt in installed hydroelectric capacity**.

"Besides, Ethiopia should remember that drought conditions are *normal* for the Sahel, in which the country is located, that's just a feature of the property," Galacti comments. "However, it's not getting better, could the hydrologic cycle be responsible? And who changed this cycle?"

Climate Change and the Hydrologic Cycle

Severe weather changes due to human-made global warming are affecting the state of the world's water, which we have all seen in disasters such as, recently, Hurricane Sandy as well as typhoons in Vietnam. Global sea levels have risen between 2 and 5 millimeters between 2007 and 2012, with a projected rise of one meter or more by 2100. The flooding from 'Superstorm' Hurricane Sandy, we learn, was due in part to sea levels in the northeastern US rising faster than the river deltas in Southeast Asia. **Water, essential for life, has become a fierce adversary.**

Why have the oceans been rising? Let's have a look at the hydrologic cycle. **There is a significant point missing—those steps involving living beings, notably humankind.** Plants and animals do not impact the hydrologic cycle negatively; only humanity does with the construction of dams, removal of groundwater from wells, water abstraction from rivers, and the **loss of 60 percent of the wetlands in the past 100 years** (1909-2009).

"No blaming city dwellers for the run on water," Galacti announces. Worldwide water use figures show that far more significant quantities of water are used in industry (22 percent) and agriculture (70 percent) than urbanization (8 percent). In the US, Europe, China, and Mexico and **around the world, farmers are encouraged to use up 70 percent of the water that overwhelmingly goes to agriculture, resulting in waste and inefficient practices**, as the Aral Sea story in the next chapter illustrates, or risk losing vital irrigation.

The café offers a *bumper crop* of corn for tortillas, papayas, grapes, strawberries, the *fruits* of this water usage.

The Aral Sea Story – Misuse of Water

The Aral Sea is just one example of water shortage and humanity's role in wasting this prime commodity.

The Aral Sea Story

"Next on the menu, food from Kazakhstan and Uzbekistan, and water from the Aral Sea, and souvenir T-shirts for everyone," Galacti says, as the structure of the Water Cycle Café expands to accommodate the ancient lake. The problem is, **the Aral Sea is shrinking**, its water pumped out of the Water Cycle Café into cotton fields worked by Uzbekistan farmers.

One of less than twenty existing ancient lakes in the world, the Aral Sea borders Uzbekistan and Kazakhstan. Still, its impact is significant: Like the **drying up of Lake Chad**, once one of the largest lakes in the world, straddling Niger, Chad, and Sudan, the shrinking of the Aral Sea has **complicated other problems of the region.**

During the past 60 years, the Aral Sea has diminished to one-fifth of its historic size and former volume. The mighty sea in our Water Cycle Café fractures into **three smaller bodies of water totaling 13,000 square kilometers**—ponds compared to the Aral Sea's **64,500 square kilometers in 1957.** Kazakhstan has turned the Northern Aral Sea around, and whereas its shoreline was 100 kilometers from the port of Aralsk, it is now only 20-25 km away, depending on the season of the year.

In Uzbekistan, **cotton farmers[1] and cotton producers have withdrawn and diverted the waters** (much as the ancient Khmer did) through a network of channels to produce cotton, their national *oqoltyn* (white gold), for international export and local livelihood. In essence, Uzbekistan is one of the world's leading cotton fiber manufacturers, along with India, China, America, and Pakistan.

The fate of the Aral Sea water goes something like this: the water diverts to soak the cotton fields for fibers to make T-shirts like the one Galacti is wearing, which takes 2,720 liters of water to produce. As **changes in the Aral Sea alter weather patterns**, the growing season for cotton shrinks to 170 days (200 days are average), endangering the cotton crops as unproductive farmland increases.

As a side effect of wasting water, **desertification converts 45,000 square kilometers of land to barren waste that yields 100 million tons of saline-laden dust. It creeps into the lungs of children and livestock**, causing pneumonia in the youngsters and suffocating cattle.

---

1. http://www.centralasia-travel.com/en/countries/uzbekistan/natural_blessings/cotton

In Aralsk, Kazakhstan and Muynak, Uzbekistan, towns on the Uzbekistan-Kazakhstan border, villagers with respiratory illnesses, anemia, kidney and liver diseases, cancer, and tuberculosis from drinking polluted water, leave their homeland in hopes of reversing worsening health.

The story is a little more encouraging as we look to the southwest of the Aral Sea and change the *menu*.

Israeli Conservation

In Israel, the **significant sources of water, such as the Sea of Galilee and the Coastal Aquifer**, which provide fifty percent of the water to Israeli households, **were mismanaged.** In essence, lead and other pollutants seeped into drinking water; dead fish lined dry bed areas of rivers, sea pollution closed beaches. A growing population increased the demand for water and decreased the water available for agriculture. Thirty-three years ago, the problem was so severe farmers faced losing their farms. At present, **Israel has reversed its national trend of pollution, salination, and overconsumption of water**. The country's Water Authority and significant companies located in Israel have worked in concert to correct the water deficiency and misuse.

The country now **recycles 80 percent of its wastewater** or 400 million cubic meters. Using the figure of 1600 cubic meters of water per ton of cereal grains, specifically wheat, it is enough to produce 250,000 short tons of grain. That's nearly a quarter of all domestic wheat consumption in Israel from 2011-2012 (900,000 tons).

Although drought is challenging the nation's wheat production, Israel is the only nation that has doubled its water productivity in agriculture, reducing its per-hectare water use in its crop fields by 37 percent and **using highly treated wastewater for irrigation**. Also, seawater **desalination plants transform water from the Mediterranean into potable** water and treat brackish groundwater. Israel's water reclamation success is so great that it now **sells water-cleaning tablets to UNICEF,** which uses them in humanitarian aid to Syria.

We eat Israeli wheat at the café to celebrate Israel's accomplishments. However, even with this positive news, we view sobering visuals of **experts predicting in 2009 that in 50 years, the world's water supply will collapse,** can we possibly *create* water, and from what?

Making More Water

The Water Cycle Café offers a demonstration of **water bottles that can create water from evaporation and condensation in the air,** as well as other nifty inventions.

Scientists have extended their imagination globally to **address the problem of water shortages.** First, a collaboration by a corporation involving scientists in America and Ireland is creating a **nanotechnology bottle that extracts water from the air** to refill itself, based on the biology of the Namib Desert beetle in Africa. However, in operation now, the *Waterboy*, an American invention, is extracting water from the air in Manila, Philippines.

The US-Philippines team has chosen Manila because plastic water bottles clog the drainage systems in the city, disrupting the water cycle and causing major flooding during typhoon season. To address this problem, the **WaterBoy takes condensation/vapor from the air to produce water, cutting down on 11,000 half-liter plastic bottles** that would otherwise wind up in landfills and drains. That's **enough bottles to build almost two *bottle schools* (two classrooms each) using plastic bottles** and other construction materials in Guatemala and El Salvador, half a world away from the Philippines. While the *bottle schools*, conceived of as a way to productively reuse throwaway plastic, can educate and assist, a better option might be to eliminate the trash.

What about the water we do have? What are we doing with it? Aside from industrial uses, water[2] has three main functions in human life: **transport**, **cleansing**, and **nourishing** (this includes animals, crops, and drinking water).

2. https://theexplanation.com/planet-water-our-cocoon-survival-beauty/

Sea or a Giant Garbage Patch

Global Yearly Plastic Input from Rivers into Oceans

The Champion

The Culprit

And the Winner is ...

Vegetable patch or garbage patch? We'll take the former anytime. But, humankind is creating the latter in our oceans, of all places.

Garbage patch of plastic. Simply put, **water transports more than ocean vessels[1]—in plants and in most living creatures it carries nutrients, chemical reactions take place through water transport, and water facilitates travel.** One of the functions of a river is to transport nutrients and minerals and raw metals in sediment, such as tin, gold, calcium, platinum, silica, salt deposits, and so forth to the soil and to oceans and lakes, similar to the way water in the body functions.

---

1. https://theexplanation.com/vital-water-transports-nourishes-cleanses-all-our-life-needs/

However, humankind's **inventiveness** and ability have **transformed these same raw materials into usable commodities** like various forms of temperature resistant, resilient, and dense plastics. Our rivers and waterways now transport a numerous variety of products of our throwaway societies around the world.

When it comes to plastic objects—you name it, we even now have 3D printers creating replacement body parts—not just for cars but for the human body. Coupled with this, we've developed more **ways to divert water, such as pipes and canals, which transport our sewage and junk via streams and rivers.** Ultimately, reaching deltas and estuaries only to wash out to sea where the saltwater both breaks this trash into minuscule irrecoverable size chunks as well as swelling our garbage laden oceans.

The Garbage Patch Nation

"The ocean currents transport stuff that ancient peoples could not have dreamed," Galacti says. "Shipwrecks and debris were common, and cargo and debris washed up onshore. But now, with globalization, **you can transport plastic bottles, which would have been unheard of a century or two ago.**"

In this Water Cycle Café, we are standing on top of an island made of plastic water bottles as well as other synthetic detritus. We are looking at the **infamous Great Pacific Garbage Patch**, also called the North Pacific Gyre or the Great North Pacific Vortex. Galacti notes there are five such expanses of waste in the world, including the Great Pacific Garbage Patch, the Indian Ocean Garbage Patch, North Atlantic Garbage Patch, a.k.a. The Sargasso Sea. The North Pacific Gyre is estimated to be anywhere from **the size of Texas to almost twice the area of continental United States.**

UNESCO has designated them collectively as **a symbolic federal state called** *Garbage Patch*[2]. These garbage patches/gyres are *plastic smorgasbords* of water bottles, beach balls, plastic forks, DV cases, Styrofoam containers, plastic bags, and other trash blown into the ocean from landfills or even dumped overboard by oceangoing ships.

Although plastic endures, its components break down rapidly in water. Galacti points to a Styrofoam container and, with his microscopic vision, observes its polystyrene molecules, heavier than the water molecules, **break down and dissolve in the ocean, creating small fragments called nurdles**. Most of the plastic, however, can last for decades or longer.

We feel buried in all this plastic, about 50,000 pieces of trash per one square mile of the ocean or given the 614,517,609 square miles of ocean, 7 trillion penny-sized fragments of debris or enough to fill the U.S. Sears Tower three times. What does this avalanche of plastic mean for the water, for animals, and humans?

Consider fish and birds such as the albatross. Albatross chicks in the Pacific **ingest five tons of objects such as a plastic cigarette lighter from Japan, a plastic child's toy, and bottle caps.** As a result, many of these chicks die because of the space the plastic takes up in their stomach. Or, they have punctured lungs and ingest harmful chemicals that attach to the trash.

As for the fish, primarily small filter feeders such as herring, tilapia, and goldfish, they suck in the nurdles, about the size of fish food pellets. In so doing, they ingest all the harmful chemicals such as BPA, PCBs, and phthalates, which kill the fish or change their sex from male to female and vice versa. If the fish survive their phthalate (cancer-causing chemical) diet, **the plastic toxins get passed on to birds, larger fish, sharks, and humans who consume fish.**

---

2. *http://www.occasionalplanet.org/2013/04/22/garbage-patch-nation/*

Ocean Cleanup

In 2013 a visionary 18-year-old, Boyan Slat, launched Ocean Cleanup[3], an organization dedicated to ridding the Oceans of the truckload of plastic, specifically targeting these monstrous garbage patches.

They have developed technology with buoys and skirts to garner vast quantities of this trash and concentrate it for easier removal, bringing it onshore for treatment and recycling into needed raw materials. Ocean Cleanup has done many tests in the North Sea, where oceanic conditions are much more severe than in the Pacific. **The first experimental cleanup system was deployed in the Pacific in September 2018.** After testing, they validated the concept, and it is now in phase two of producing a second system based on lessons learned. The least that can be said is here's a concerted effort to try to overcome this blight.

We can't put the responsibility for trash and pollution in the ocean solely on seafarers. The vast majority of the plastic is disposed of or tossed away on land. **We add some 5,000 tons of plastic solids, the equivalent weight of 65 space shuttles, to the oceans every day.** Now it's time not only to start removing it but also to stop feeding the garbage patch.

Is the bottle half-full or half-empty, or in this case, are the world's oceans getting trashier or cleaner?

---

3. https://theoceancleanup.com/

Wastewater or Chemically Cleaned Water

Bathing and cleansing in wastewater—what a paradox. Unfortunately, a reality in poorer countries around the world. Is the glass half-full or half-empty?

Is our worldwide water supply headed towards wastewater or clean water? It's sad that we even have to ask or think about such a question. But there are huge organizations devoted to just this cause.

Cleansing

From the kitchen in the Water Cycle Café, we watch village women bathing and washing in the Irrawaddy River in the country of Myanmar (Burma). While baths and bathrooms are the norms for much of the world, **in several nations** such as India, Myanmar, China, and several Africa countries, **river bathing and washing are frequent.**

Remember when you were a child swimming in *the old swimming hole* or a nearby river or lake? Remember that clean, refreshing feeling from the water[1]? In Western societies, in Asia and the Middle East, **bathing and showering are a necessity, part of proper grooming**, cleanliness, and hygiene. In essence, the Japanese often cleanse themselves in sex-segregated hot springs or onsen.

If we ask most of our tour group what the **greatest inventions of humankind are, plumbing is high** on, if not the top, of the list. Galacti passes out replicas of the earliest known ancient earthenware plumbing pipes (2700 BC), reinforced with asphalt to guard against leaks, used by the Indus River Valley civilization.

We visit, via the café, **Borobudur Temple in Indonesia and view the ancient restored plumbing** in the temple. We pull up a keystone and see the drainage pipes that connect to the 8th-century crocodile and dragon statues, which, like ornamental but functional **gargoyle water spouts** on Notre-Dame de Paris, in France, and on Greek temples, **drain the excess water or wastewater** from the temple. In the throne room of Borobudur, the ancient Indonesians placed the nexus of the water drainage system. All of this facilitates the cleansing of the temple and the people.

"So, is there anything *wrong* with this emphasis on cleanliness?" Galacti wonders. "Certainly, bathing is necessary for health. But I wonder, does everyone have access to clean water for washing and the toilette?"

---

1. https://theexplanation.com/planet-water-our-cocoon-survival-beauty/

We've gone from cleansing being a necessity, with universal **access to enough clean water** being the ideal, to countries having to be aware of wasting water in bathing. For example, the average UK citizen taking a daily **eight-minute power shower** uses around 136 liters/29 UK gallons of hot water, or **16 liters** *a minute*. In contrast, the total amount of water an **African family** uses in a day is **23 liters** *a day* (8300 liters per year).

Many African countries have no running water to shower or wash in. Instead, in countries such as Kenya, Malawi, Zambia, and Uganda, the people have created a household device called a *tippy-tap*, a bottle attached to a tree by a string. A makeshift foot pedal activates the water flow for washing hands—one of these devices is available for us to examine at the café. We find it does the job but takes a lot of effort.

In 2012 over 100,000 households in Kenya, Malawi and Zambia made *tippy-taps* because there was no option to install plumbing and sinks. If you contrast this with a London home in which a sink with running water is the norm, the *tippy-tap*, while a workable solution, just **shows the inequities.** How did the situation get this way? Which reminds us: we're talking mainly clean water, **what about countries in which people bathe in filthy wastewater?**

The Ganges River in India flows through the café, allowing us to observe an astonishing ritual. **Benares** (Varanasi), considered by Hindus to be the most sacred city in India, is crowded with corpses on rafts and with fecal matter. Human waste leaks into the river; however, the Hindus still float their decomposing dead on rafts in the water and then **bathe ceremonially in the polluted wastewater.** Hindus traditionally place great significance on bathing in the Ganges or coming to India's holiest city to die, be cremated, and floated in the Ganges.

According to figures, Hindu Brahmins (priests) and mourners in **Hindu death rituals release 35,000 bodies into the river each year**[2] since crematoriums are in disrepair and cannot handle the sheer numbers of bodies. Imagine the stench of decomposition in the water, the bacteria and diseases released.

Yes, this practice is essential in a religious sense, but **is water quality sacrificed?** The Ganges mysteriously *clouds* this issue by seemingly *cleansing itself* of bacteria, for example, eliminating a strain of Escherichia *coli* (*E.coli*) in three days, as scientific experiments have proven. Scientists think this mysterious phenomenon may be attributed to macrophages eating bacteria or the river's high oxygenation, for example.

However, the river's *cleansing* properties face a challenge because of progress, namely **dam construction to supply hydroelectric power to India.** Because India suffered a blackout in 2012 that left 2 percent of the country's 1.2 billion people without power and is third in fossil-fuel carbon dioxide emissions in the world, the Indian government plans 300 such projects near the Himalayan glaciers in the north of India. Yet **the dams' filtration system will interfere with the natural water flow, therefore reducing the river's ability to *renew itself.***

Furthermore, the hydroelectric power generated by the dams by 2030 will amount to 100,000 MW, or 6 percent of the country's energy needs, or **enough to power the national capital territory of Delhi** (the world's fourth-largest city) **for 29 days** (Delhi's average power demand is 3,500 MW per day).

Adding to the problem, **Varanasi lacks a stable electricity supply. It thus cannot run wastewater treatment plants to cleanse the water** of the decomposing bodies, fecal matter, and 40-78 percent of city waste that makes its way from the streets of Varanasi into the water supply.

---

2. http://www.outlookindia.com/article.aspx?277355:

What we have here is bathing taken to its extreme—cleansing that is not genuinely cleansing because of pollution and diversion of water. Yes, generating more renewable energy is desirable in a surging population, but as with the Ethiopian dam, there are costs.

There are many other Ganges situations in the world, and they don't all involve bathing. More strikingly, they include not being able to satisfy an even more fundamental human function. Galacti notes that according to UN statistics, 2.6 billion people, or **1/3 of the world's population and twice the population of China, lack toilet facilities**. In many countries worldwide, more people have a mobile phone than a toilet.

Why are we concerned about this?

Pollution

The oceans cover 71 percent of the Earth's surface and contain 1,460,000,000 tons of water. If we piled it on the visible land, it would reach 1,100 km high! That's into outer space; not even planes fly that high. If you dropped a bottle of ink in such a volume within seconds, it would dissipate, never to be seen again. It's **hard to imagine that such an amount could be contaminated. Well, it's headed in that direction**. We have to *treat freshwater chemically* to use it.

Fluoride, Chlorine, Chemical Treatment

The tap water you use today, the pool you swim in, everything you eat or use that contains water (most goods), all of these are likely altered by chlorine and chloramine. Water needs *disinfection* of bacteria and pollutants for human consumption and use—it also needs to be *filtered* and *distilled*.

Joining the exhibits in the Water Cycle Café is a chlorinated swimming pool.

Chlorine has purified water, but the question is: are those chemicals beneficial? Chlorine kills bacteria and other contaminants by breaking down the cell walls of the bacteria through acids and ions, and if you drink it for a long time, you may become ill.

Environmental Contamination

Next up for inspection is the **Huang He or Yellow River or _Mother River_ in Northern Chin[3]a**, whose delta is 36,272 square kilometers, slightly larger than the Netherlands. It provides water for 12 percent of China's 1.3 billion population and 15 percent of its farmland; this is not just the source of water diverted during the Beijing Summer Olympics. It's **the birth of Chinese civilization, its lower portion is home to 1.9 million people, and now it is the polluted Mother River of China.**

From fishermen in small boats that coexist with factory emissions, to villagers taking samples of waters that run red because of the pollution, the people must share **a one-third unusable water supply.** Besides, the population is distressed because the Yellow River is drying up, and coal companies are diverting more water from it since 85 percent of China's coal lies in that region.

The water that remains gets polluted by **80 million tons of mostly untreated wastewater from the coal mines**, every year—to put this in perspective, 80 million tons of sewage would fill 3200 Olympic swimming pools. Visualize all that waste choking the Yellow River. While not quite an _open-pit toilet_ compared to several rivers (including the Ganges), the Yellow River and its condition have troubled Chinese citizens, environmental groups, and scientists worldwide.

---

3. http://europe.chinadaily.com.cn/china/2013-03/31/content_16361917.htm

Remember the example of Erin Brockovich, who called attention to the pollution of water with chromium-6 in the USA. Worldwide, voices are speaking about ecology, such as, in the case of the Yellow River. International agencies and even water companies such as Veolia and Thames/RWE and government officials in China, and Greenpeace have been **airing concerns since 2006 about the water in the Yellow River being undrinkable**.

Is there a solution to pollution? Governments have tried: the Malaysian government imposed the death penalty on would-be polluters, and China has unveiled a similar measure.

Yes, the situation is that dire, Galacti says. Worldwide, water sources such as rivers in the UK, where 40 percent of otters test positive for the flu-like illness Toxoplasmosis that is particularly deadly to people with HIV and weakened immune systems. Egypt's Nile River, which carries 60 percent of rural waste disposal and 40 percent of urban waste disposal, is responsible for 17,000 children dying of dysentery each year. Water-borne diseases such as dysentery and diarrhea are killing more children than malaria or HIV.

There must be some more *positive* news, and there is, just in time for lunch, which we have as the café transforms into a restaurant in Cambodia.

Nourishing Water or Dead Zones

Water, the natural habitat of fish, sustains one billion people on our planet.

We might tend to shy away from this slithery nourishment, but for many, it is life. A ship (encircled in the image) leaves a wake as it plows through Baltic Sea dead zone algae, A Khmer fishing village with an abundant catch of nourishing fish. What are we doing with our water?

Life in a Cambodian Fishing Village

We are floating on the Tonle Sap River in Cambodia, observing the traditional lake/river village floating houses built of bamboo and anchored by boats, also made of bamboo. As well as a boat market where the residents set up the houses for selling, as well as a floating gym, battery shops, and medical clinic. **We watch the daily life of the Cambodian or Khmer *lake-dwellers*,** who have been building their floating homes, living on the lake, fishing, and growing rice for food. The Khmer fishermen harvest fish from the lake's 150 species of fish in the same manner their ancestors did a thousand years ago.

They use the traditional large bamboo baskets to fish, as well as smaller baskets to harvest tiny shrimp. The fishermen submerge their fish and shrimp traps overnight, anchoring the shrimp baskets to trees. As the water fills the bamboo basket traps, so, too, do fish fill the baskets. When the fishermen draw the basket traps from the river the next morning, the small and large baskets are brim-full with shrimp and fish, respectively, packed together as you can see in this video[1].

Traditionally Khmer people, Cambodian people, are farmers and fishermen and rice-growers; the urban planning in the ancient city of Angkor, which once supported 1 million people, **was based on water technology**; unfortunately, *poor stewardship* **used up that water and the Khmer abandoned it**. The farmers follow the seasons and the regime of water. Still, Galacti observes that they also obey government regulations and avoid catching shrimp from June to September, the shrimp-breeding season.

The fishermen obey Order 001 and do not fish from July to October. Otherwise, the government burns the fish traps, fishing tools, and shrimp baskets! **Family fish farms** (aquaculture) assist in the food supply for raising fish and tiny shrimp. Indeed, the lake has been historically responsible for feeding an empire.

The lake made the building of Angkor Wat and all other magnificent Khmer temples possible, since the rice paddies, watered by the lake and fed by the reservoirs, could feed the 300,000 people who built Angkor Wat in 30 years. Also, the lake is **a source of food**. We see a history re-

1. https://youtu.be/w9uR7yiauVs

view of the ancient Khmer people in 800 AD, settling in this area rich with water resources coupled with the supply of building material in the mountains and forests (stone for the temples, wood for houses) and additional food sources, such as wild game, in the forest.

We notice from watching the historical review that **the ancient Khmer exist in harmony with the water just as their *modern* counterparts do.** Their modern counterparts have cell phones made by a company in Vietnam, and the houseboats have battery-powered televisions. Still, the modern Khmer and the ancient Khmer both let their bamboo houses move with the tide rather than radically changing their environment to suit them.

It is thought-provoking to see a culture live peacefully with nature on the lake[2], in a country with a complicated recent past. Even though there has been deforestation affecting the Tonle Sap River and Lake in Cambodia, the fishing solution seems to work well as opposed to *dead zones* worldwide.

Extremes: "Dead Zones"

As we look at the photos we have taken of the Tonle Sap fishing village; our boat takes us into **one of the 500 dead zones of oceans and seas on the planet[3].** Most of which we find along the eastern coast of the United States, and the coastlines of the Baltic States, Japan, and the Korean Peninsula. The Baltic Sea, in particular, is thought to be the world's largest *death zone.*

The Baltic Sea, which borders Poland, Germany, Russia, Finland, Denmark, Sweden, Estonia, Latvia, and Lithuania, is called **the world's most polluted sea.** It is not just the 60,000 tons of World War II-era mustard gas and arsenic, lying dormant in a military wreck that *might*

---

2. https://theexplanation.com/coastal-zones-home-to-forty-percent-of-world-population/

3. http://neptune911.wordpress.com/2013/08/23/over-500-oceanic-dead-zones-counted/

be released and contaminate the water. **It's that contaminated bilge-water, oil spills, wastewater treatment runoff, and industrial waste that have been a problem in the Baltic since 2002.** And now, the *dead zone* is as large as the entire border state of Latvia.

Simply put, a *dead zone* **is a section of water in which pollution causes mass algae blooms**; in turn, the **algae remove all the oxygen** supply needed by the fish and other marine life—the result is **fish dying off.** Dead cod and whiting rot in the open air while trawlers and fishing boats continue to catch them. **Plants such as eelgrass, necessary to cleanse nitrogen from the water of the Baltic Sea, die because of the elimination of their oxygen** by a concentration of hazardous substances. These pollutants are twenty times greater than, for example, in the North Atlantic dead zones on the Eastern US/Canada and Western European Atlantic coasts.

To explore the pollution damage from these substances, international teams conduct deep-water surveys of Baltic marine fauna: blue jellyfish, hermit crabs, Atlantic butterfish, Baltic cod, and colorful young sea snails. Unfortunately, dead white blue jellyfish, as well as other sea creatures, have gone *belly up*. **In addition to pollution, overfishing of Baltic cod triggers an *algae bloom storm*,** since Baltic cod eat herring (sprats), which eat zooplankton, which eats algae. In short: fewer Baltic cod leads to more sprats, fewer zooplankton, and more algae.

Algal blooms threaten human life when washed up on Baltic Sea coastlines and beaches such as Sopot in Poland and the shores of Gotland in Sweden. **Swimmers in these waters and young children playing on the algae dumps on the beach experience severe health problems:** skin and eye irritations, allergic reactions, gastrointestinal upset, serious illness, and death.

What to do to correct the damage? Well, it is difficult; unlike most lakes and seas, the Baltic Sea has too much volume of water to be oxygenated or dredged for trash and chemicals as land-locked lakes are. The Baltic Sea problem is so pervasive that Russia, Finland, and ten other Baltic and European nations, including Poland, which has its own ideas, have met to promote biodiversity[4]. They want to reduce pollution from ships, and in keeping with this, eliminate the 49,000 square kilometers morass of algae that originally choked the waters of the Baltic in 2010.

The Baltic States reported that the algae blooms are due in part to annual emissions of 36,000 British metric tonnes of phosphorus and 737,000 tonnes of nitrogen. **To achieve this goal, the Baltic and other European states need to reduce those emissions by 15,000 tonnes of phosphorus and 135,000 tonnes of nitrogen annually.** According to the latest report, because of measures such as improving wastewater treatment plants and sludge treatment in Riga and Jurmala, Latvia, Gdansk, Poland, Brest, Belarus, and Turku, Finland, concrete commitments are underway for change.

Finland is using the mineral gypsum in the fields to reduce the leaching of dangerous chemicals. How does gypsum do this? Well, this mineral changes the structure of soils, especially acid sandy soils (which Finland has), and inhibits leaching of phosphorus, for example. That solution is less than successful in **Poland: a large phosphor-gypsum waste pile in Gdansk**, which is slowly leaking, could **release more chemicals into the water than all of the disposal sites located near Finland's cities combined**.

Shipwrecks as a Solution

4. https://www.ncbi.nlm.nih.gov/pmc/articles/PMC4832911/

Fishermen in these dead zones trawl for fish on the floor in the depths, wrecking the habitat and crushing, snaring, or leaving vulnerable the fish that escape the boats. In many cases, there are no more fish, or fishing is banned entirely. Species diversity decreases, although different species may make the wrecked habitat their new home. **Annually, deep-bottom trawling worldwide destroys a seabed area twice the size on the continental United States**—the very dry seabed on which we are standing.

Shipwrecks and sinking old hulks cause them to calcify into coral reefs. It is deliberate, and mariners, in some cases, wreck ships to encourage new coral reefs. The shipwrecks have two significant complementary effects: providing homes for all manner of fish, crustaceans and other sea life, and helping invasive species to grow.

A program in the USA, mainly in the Gulf of Mexico, called **Rigs-for-reefs, considers that the offshore oil platforms are already artificial reefs,** having been in place ten and up to 30 or 40 years. Marine life concentrates around them, and the project simply reduces their height or topples them over—a way to protect and promote the environment that nourishes so many people worldwide.

Water Resources, Coral Reefs & Soda

Water resources cover the entire range of human activities. From recreation, thirst-quenching, bathing, and crop production. It is a commodity we cannot forgo. Humans need clean water.

Coral Reef Destruction

A 41 percent increase of carbon dioxide in the atmosphere since 1990 is **causing its excessive dissolving and the formation of carbonic acid in the oceans.** A study by Timothy Wootton of the University of Chicago revealed that this is happening ten times faster than simulations expected. The result *of the saltwater* is an *increase in acidity 23 times more than predicted,* which can disrupt marine life.

The acidity or pH, which is 8.1 (Galacti shows us that the neutral pH level is 7), has **already started to attack billions of carbonate calcium shells of marine organisms in all oceans around the world**. The acidity is causing *osteoporosis* in coral reef polyps, which, when alive, provide an essential part of the marine food chain (feeding on small animals) and shelter for clownfish, raccoon fish, blue tang, and eels, for example. **When the coral polyps die, their skeletons build the Great Barrier Reef or the coral reefs of the Hawaiian Islands.**

There is another reason to care about the coral reefs and pollution, if not just for ethics' sake or as humanitarians: for health reasons. **Many pharmaceuticals are being developed from the diversity and extraordinary resistance of reef-dwelling marine life**[1].

Pepsico, Voss, and Shoes for Water

We learn that drinkable, **clean water resources are a scarce commodity for some 780 million people worldwide**, 2.5 times the population of the United States. They lack access to improved water resources; this affects approximately one in nine people. Two-thirds of Africa lack access to drinkable water and some Middle Eastern countries must import 90% of their drinking water.

Who is acting to reverse this trend? Will international organizations such as church groups, charities, and even corporations provide drinkable water to *water-stressed* parts of the world such as sub-Saharan Africa, Haiti, South America, and so on? Well, yes, companies such as TOMS Shoes and Voss Water, as well as charities such as Shoeman Wa-

---

1. https://theexplanation.com/coastal-zones-home-to-forty-percent-of-world-population/

ter Projects, are all using **commerce as a vehicle to fund water projects** such as clean-water wells in Ethiopia and drinking water in a school in Haiti.

What are the concrete results, as we drink bottles of Voss water and wear pairs of TOMS shoes, specifically sold to raise funds for water resources projects? **These corporate-charity partnerships have funded more than 8,000 projects**, helping bring clean and safe drinking water to more than 3.2 million people in twenty countries.

Sodas and Corporate Water Privatization

Ah, but for every corporate project intended to ease water stress, we have the reach of *globalization* using up more resources. That picture is changing, thanks to factories such as one owned by Pepsico in India. Pepsico reduced overall water consumption in its plants by 20 percent in 2015. Already **Pepsico conserves more water resources than its actual plants consume** via water regeneration programs. It has saved 16 billion liters of water from 2006 to 2011, with an additional 45 percent reduction in water consumption in India from the 2005 base. But India is facing severe water contamination and shortage because of agriculture and lack of monsoon precipitation.

However, **corporations also buy up water resources from countries and sell water back to the people in bottled water** form or manage the water as they please. In France, the companies Suez/Veolia had a bottled water monopoly and free access to Paris water until Paris voted to reclaim its water services. As a digression, bottled water serves a purpose, especially in so many countries in which you have to boil the water and sterilize it to drink it. However, again, let's **question *why* the waterways of Kuala Lumpur, Jakarta, Buenos Aires, or Acapulco are in such a poor state** that we can't even brush our teeth in a hotel bathroom.

The debate over bottled water misses this fundamental point—and there is plenty to debate over. Many parks under the umbrella of the U.S. National Park Service have eliminated bottled water from all these international tourist spots such as the Grand Canyon, Zion National Park in Utah, and Hawaii Volcanoes National Park.

So **why do organizations such as the World Bank continue to fund private water companies** such as Suez/Veolia and Thames/RWE, which appropriate water from communities worldwide and do not do the job of providing water services in the Philippines, for example?

Corporations and states do come to a mutual compromise that is *benevolent*. For example, in September 2017, Southwestern water and the U.S. government confirmed the U.S.-Mexican agreement for sharing the distressed Colorado River water. The U.S. will invest in the vicinity of $31.5 million to support Mexico's water infrastructure and upgrade their farmland production. In exchange, Mexico agreed to reduce its portion of river allotment should the U.S. reduce its own water allotment in case of severe shortages, because of drought conditions.

Regional water agencies bought another 1.9 billion cubic meters of water (enough to support the bathing, washing, and nourishing needs of 200,000 families for a year) from Mexico's share of the Colorado River in Southern California, Arizona, and Nevada for $10 million. That amount is destined to repair irrigation canals on farms in Mexico. Also, the compromise involves selling Colorado water back to Mexico at a later date. To Mexican farmers in Mexicali who want the canal restoration, the agreement seems worthwhile.

It brings us full circle back to the land and crops and water resources.

We have seen how Israel has smartened its water practices, but other countries have their own processes for recycling and reusing water. In the areas surrounding Mexico City, **the wastewater is all that is avail-**

able to the farmers, who use the tainted water to grow crops. We shake our heads as we realize we cannot eat particular fruit that comes from Mexico or markets in Taiwan or China.

In these countries, the term *organic* does not take into consideration *environmental contamination*, only, no use of immediate and locally used products like fertilizers and pesticides. The earth and the water might be polluted, and produce can still be exported and marketed—which is the case. What's **in the water winds up in our food**.

We take a drink from a clear crystal stream, and we view the ability to cleanse, bathe, have free access to water from our sink or a glass, sail the oceans, and harness hydroelectric power as a *glass-half-full getting fuller*. We look at waste disposal, chemical dumping, and poor management as a *glass-half-empty getting emptier*.

4. Audit Land

Fertile Farmland or Desert

Fertile farmland is a primary concern worldwide. Countries in North Africa bordering the Sahara are learning to push it back with the Great Green Wall.

We consider the Earth once again.

Earth is like an apple of fire and pressure with a skin capable of supporting life. Its crust is a narrow band of comfortable temperature on a tiny ball, in a limited habitable orbital range around a sun. **A pinpoint speck of the universe supports everything we eat, do, create, and dream.** Savannas, forests, farmland, swamps, and deserts house all the people, plants, and animals of the Earth. Swatches of the land grow all the food we eat. The rocks beneath provide every raw material necessary to support our endeavors and industries.

With a wave of his hand, our guide Galacti moves our perspective to several hundred miles above the Earth.

"I like much of what you have done with the place," he says, experimenting with human slang, which he seems to find amusing. "**You have found abundance in even the remotest areas**, and turned those resources into creations even a being like me finds impressive."

"Thank you," I say on behalf of all humankind. "We do try."

"You have even flung parts of this Earth far away, cast them out into space to find new lands to inhabit. Or should I say conquer?"

Another wave of Galacti's hand and portions of the globe glow a warm, comforting green. "Here," he says, pointing to the cities of Abu Dhabi, Las Vegas, and Bombay. "Here **you have turned desert into paradise through nothing but the ingenuity of your minds and the works of your hands**. And here he indicates cities on the Italian coast, beaches in Malaysia and expansive farmland in Denmark and Holland "you have captured land from the sea itself."

A third wave and the green disappears, replaced by blotches of angry red scattered across the globe. "**But your accomplishments have come at a cost**. You have turned the lush jungle into a desert, former farmland into waste, entire lakes into poison. Though these are also impressive in their own way, I wonder at the wisdom of it."

I think to explain that those scars on the land are not intentional, that they are but side products of the wonders Galacti mentioned, but I realize he already knows that.

"Both are true," I say instead.

"Let us look closer," Galacti retorts. "**You have accomplished much and have proven you can repair much of what you break** in your race to make those accomplishments. In the end, have you done more good or more harm to this fragile home of yours?"

Land: Supporting Human Life

Land is supremely valuable to us humans[1]. Except for a few dozen astronauts, everything humankind has ever done, seen, felt tasted, or smelled comes from the Land. We sense that value when we step from a plane or a boat onto the earth. Our language itself underscores the importance with phrases like *on solid ground* or *salt of the earth* describing safe situations and trustworthy individuals.

From a human perspective, **our most important use of land is agriculture**. Without farmland and the food that it brings us, nothing else we attempt would be possible for longer than it takes to die of hunger.

Agricultural Advancement

The first real use we humans made of the Land was to **eat the food that grew from it**. After a time, inhabitants of the Earth moved from eating what they found to producing what they ate. Later, this change led to the formation of cities, specialized experts, and technological advancement.

Early man learned **the basics of agrarian farming**, how to plant with the cycles of the seasons, to fertilize our fields with the remains of previous crops, and to rotate crops in ways that kept the areas fertile and productive. In the East, cultures growing rice discovered that keeping fish in their rice paddies fertilized the soil while simultaneously reducing pests and increasing a population of natural protein sources.

---

1. https://theexplanation.com/land-surface-temperature-just-right-for-your-bare-feet/

The Netherlands, of which 1/8th is below sea level, first farmed on artificial hillocks. They later built a system of dikes that protected the region's flood plains and made the area habitable and arable. Most of the region wouldn't exist without that network to keep the saltwater sea away. It provides over 11,000 square kilometers—the area of Jamaica—of arable land the Dutch use to feed themselves and export food to other nations.

Disappearing Farmland

You don't see the word *desertification* much on the news, but it is a significant crisis that results from our use of the land. The term means agricultural land that becomes unsuitable for farming, often changing into barren rock or arid waste. A June 2009 report by the United Nations identified desertification, amplified by global climate change, as the most significant environmental challenge of the current epoch.

We discussed the Aral Sea in the previous chapter as one example of the speedy, accelerating pace of human-caused desertification. Lake Tchad in Africa is another. Between 1970 and 2010, the lake shrunk from 25,000 square kilometers to only 5,000, due to a combination of water over-usage and reduced precipitation to refill the lake. The entire body of water is in real danger of vanishing and, with it, the ability to farm for every community at its edge.

According to UN reports, approximately 1/3 of the human population live in arid zones, and 60 million inhabitants of Subsaharan Africa have had to leave their homes because the water supply no longer supports local farming.

"You consume more than you create, and it leads to suffering. You can say it was unintended, but you can't pretend it was not forewarned," Galacti says.

"But we solve our problems," I object. "If we do anything well, it's rising to the occasion and overcoming trouble."

"That is true," he responds. As he speaks, a warm green line appears in sections along the southern border of the world's largest and most famous desert.

The **Great Green Wall movement emerged as an attempt to curb desertification in Subsaharan Africa** by developing and planting genetically engineered trees that grow roots quickly and require very little water to thrive. Workers plant these trees along the border of the desert, where they take root and begin fixing arable soil in place. **The Wall** *holds the line* **against the advancing desert**, and stage two will plant a second Wall advancing *into* the Sahara. This movement spans multiple countries and required cooperation among numerous scientific disciplines and the breadth of a continent. It is truly a wondrous project that celebrates the best of what humans can accomplish. This video[2] reveals the extent of the program.

As of 2017, more than 80% of the originally planted trees have died. You might think this has brought an end to the program.

On the contrary, it had the virtue of focusing populations on a significant problem, and human ingenuity has now come to play a large part in recovery and upswing. The idea is to work with and encourage nature. Planting continues, but the more significant emphasis is on working with trees that naturally sprout and grow. Indigenous knowledge of past conservation practices about water by building retaining plateaus and protecting trees and putting shrubs to better use is paramount.

"Impressive," Galacti allows, "but how often have your solutions caused their own set of problems?"

---

2. https://youtu.be/4xls7K_xFBQ

"More often than not," I admit. "But in Subsaharan Africa, headway is being made for the benefit of many communities."

Industrial Fertilizer or Organic Farming

The Land: Which way are we headed? Industrial Fertilizer or Organic Farming and Rare Earth metals

If we put the land first and make it the priority, then choices should become more straightforward. There are all sorts of opinions and debates, but is the tide turning to a saner way of eating?

Fads of the Land

Food fads happen when we place more importance on one kind of food than on others, and choose to eat out of balance with what is available or healthy. As **wheat and corn became unpopular** in Western countries, the grain **quinoa came into vogue in restaurants and bakeries.**

This transition created a boom where **prices for quinoa seed multiplied 20 times in Bolivia**, the source of nearly half the world's supply of this grain. Although this improved the quality of life for some Bolivian farmers and broadened our options at restaurants and in grocery stores, the benefit did not come without an unconsidered cost.

Quinoa demands so much water that farmers had to suspend growing on half or more of their land. This extra demand has also threatened llama farmers in the region, as well as the wild plant and animal populations. The **short-term gain has created an unstable situation that harms the land** and disrupts the human communities inhabiting it.

By happy contrast, **some farmers** in the developed world are once again **embracing organic agriculture.** Farms joining this movement end the cycle of destructive chemical farming and begin the process of rebuilding a natural population of worms and bacteria that fertilize the soil naturally. These farms have an impact on local farm life and produce food that is higher in nutrients and micronutrients than their industrially farmed counterparts. Although less than 5% of the food we provide is organic, this **might indicate an upswing tendency to rebuild the land rather than destroy it.**

Failing with Phosphorus

We once considered **phosphorus and nitrogen fertilizers the cure for hunger worldwide.** They provided the essential nutrients instantly before we had to wait for the land to regenerate them over months and years. Using these **technological marvels makes the land significantly more productive than a traditional schedule of crop rotation and natural compost.**

But that fertilizer kills the bacteria and worms that provide soil sustainability over time. As we deplete our mined reserves of **NPK** (nitrogen, phosphorus, and potassium) and those **fertilizers become more expensive**, farmers are finding it increasingly difficult to continue this *modern* farming. It takes years for chemically fertilized fields to restore their natural fertilization, meaning farmers could go broke in the interim. Diminished food supplies and displaced populations are other real risks of a breakdown in this practice of farming.

It's a question seemingly without an answer. With the absence of modern fertilizing methods, the land can feed approximately 6 billion people according to recent estimates. **Using nitrogen and phosphorus lets us feed the current and growing future populations, but puts us at risk of more significant problems.**

"It's a challenge," I admit to my companion, "but we are already rising to it."

The Other Side of Fertilization

Vittel, France, has been known for centuries as a place with pure and even curative mineral waters. Wishing to protect that asset, the **local government decided to ban the use of industrial fertilizers** and pesticides during the 1990s when scientists first started to learn about the pollution associated with them. Over the past two decades, their water sources have again become untainted by chemical contaminants and the region profits both by selling that water worldwide and with healthy agricultural practices. **All around, land quality is much improved.**

A second, though accidental example happens in **Wales**, one of the poorest parts of Great Britain. When chemical fertilizers first became popular Welsh farmers couldn't afford them. **After decades of not us-**

ing those pollutants, **Wales has the purest coastal waters in the region** and can now export both bottled water and sea salt, popular among consumers and professional chefs alike.

"It doesn't solve every problem from chemical fertilizer," I say, "but as a start, it makes for a tasty steak." An excellent example of protecting coastal zones[1] (Inventory, chapter 3), both seaside and landside.

Yes, there are plenty of examples, **encouraging and discouraging**, regarding the state of our water and land resources. When we add it all up—and come to the bottom line—**are we more on the positive or negative side of peace and prosperity? We're making an** *Audit of the Universe*.

Land: Supporting Human Endeavors

The land has not provided merely for our survival. **Mineral resources have permitted every accomplishment and creature comfort we have ever enjoyed**. We build homes of concrete and brick using mineral resources, heat our homes with coal and oil and uranium. We make tools from silex and iron, and ornaments of gold, silver, diamond, and sapphire.

Everything you buy and use is manufactured from one kind of natural resource or another, even the most technically advanced toys. Modern consumer societies have built a system around this: a cycle of creating things out of natural resources so we can buy something, somebody else created. All of it begins with using the gifts of the land.

At our best, humankind's **use of natural resources has been wondrous**. In recent years, we have developed amazing things:

- **Hydrophobic plastics** and fabrics that repel water to make

---

surfaces cleaner, safer and more resistant to corrosion
- **Glass that changes shape and texture** in response to an electrical current
- A *skin gun* **that regrows skin onto burn victims**, turning healing time from months of painful treatments with a high risk of infection to just days of recovery
- **Hand-held devices** that can understand what we say and **correct our grammar**

"These are impressive accomplishments," Galacti states, instantaneously aware of all we have accomplished for good or ill. "But I wonder: **do the costs and benefits balance out?** Or does one outweigh the other?"

Rare Earth Metals

Rare earth metals, so-called, not solely for their relative scarcity, but because they are challenging, **dangerous, and expensive to extract** from their natural home deep within the earth. Few natural resources demonstrate our ability to turn the raw materials of the land into high-tech wonders like our usage of rare earth metals.

- We turn **platinum into fuel cells** and devices to reduce pollution in cars.
- We use yttrium to create lasers, superconductors, and the filters that make microwave ovens safe for use in homes.
- **Dysprosium** and **neodymium** are in the **magnets for MRI scans** and used in building safe nuclear reactors.
- **We find Terbium in more reliable fuel cells**, many portable electronics, and sonar systems that allow us to explore the sea and the human body.
- **Lanthanum** is a critical component of every **hybrid car** on the road.
- **Promethium makes x-ray imaging**, and all of the medical

advances resulting from it, possible.

As another example of human resourcefulness, these **rare earth metals are part of the technologies we use to reduce our impact on the land**. They allow for cleaner cars, abundant energy, more efficient commerce, and reduced pollution – all using gifts of the land to improve our stewardship of the source of those gifts.

But this support may be **a short-term solution as world supplies of many rare earth metals run short**. Countries lacking these resources, researchers, and companies are scrambling to come up with viable solutions, from recycling to alternative minerals. The race is on to find more abundant sources, more efficient extraction methods, and efforts to thwart steeply rising prices for these rare earth resources.

This situation is not limited to rare earth metals. **Three-quarters of the world's phosphorus supply**, which you now know is vital for modern farming techniques feeding the world's seven billion inhabitants, **is found in Morocco**. This concentration creates a **vulnerable *choke-point*** for the world's food supply and forces both dangerous fluctuations in food prices as conditions change in this one small corner of the land.

There are two sides to each of our stories.

Recycling vs. Throw-Away Society

Waste, waste everywhere - built-in obsolescence versus recycling and more ecological use of our land resources. Which is progressing?

Many troubles with our waste come from the use of the land **not from the *amount* of available resources, but how we choose to *distribute* what is available.** As a species, we are wasteful of the land's gifts.

In the developed world, **we waste**:

- 61% of the energy generated in the United States alone (enough to power the entire UK for seven years).
- 40% to 50% of food produced for consumption.
- Thirty-five million cell phones and 350 million printer cartridges.
- Ten liters of water for each sheet of A4 paper produced.
- Seven million tons of solid waste dumped annually into the ocean.

The immense scale of our waste doesn't just come from **consumers choosing to throw things away rather than repair or fully use them.** Much comes from the producers who take raw materials from the land and craft them into our wondrous comforts.

The term *planned obsolescence* is manufacturing jargon that means building a product at a lower quality than is possible, specifically so it will break and force consumers to buy replacements rather than live with a working product. When you buy an umbrella or a pair of shoes from Walmart, they will not last as long as they might have lasted even if manufactured at the same cost. The manufacturer designed and built them to wear out so you would come back and buy a new one.

All of that waste has to go somewhere. Thalifushi Island in the Maldives is one of those places. Although called an *island*, Thalifushi is technically a **lagoon filled with rubbish** until the garbage heap has risen above sea level. The artificial landmass of some 500 thousand square meters (the area of Vatican City) is the **regional dumping ground for rubbish and food waste**, but also the **final resting place of batteries, mercury products, computer components,** and other items that leach toxins directly into the sea. Open burning on the island pollutes air for kilometers in every direction, and rubbish floats into the open sea with every outgoing tide.

More than a few unscrupulous producers, instead of using proper disposal of the waste, opt for dumping it in remote areas of the land or sea, where it seeps into the water table or causes pollution. Or, they simply **hire space in a developing nation** with a less stringent (and therefore less expensive) set of environmental laws. International agencies and action combat such antics, but it isn't easy to patrol the world.

The Best Laid Plans

Even when regulation is strict and carefully observed, human wonders can lead to unintentional disaster. The design and human errors behind the **Chernobyl nuclear disaster** rendered over 150,000 square kilometers of land **unavailable for many years**, and the epicenter will not be safe for us to re-enter for another 20 millennia. When earthquake damage opened the core of the **Fukushima** plant in Japan, radiation was detectable in small amounts as far away as Alaska and Northern California.

Even these disasters simultaneously stimulated the resourcefulness that makes us what we are at our best. A team at Michigan State University has discovered and tested **bacteria that eat radioactivity and excrete electricity** – a discovery they are even now putting to work to aid cleanup efforts at Fukushima.

Solutions for Our Solutions

In a further example of **our contradictory nature, we humans have found ways to counter the destructive effects of our mistakes.** In Africa, **solar ovens** and lamps generate light and heat without using polluting energy sources like wood and rubber or even dangerous ones like scavenged jet fuel. The **Wello venture, founded to create a wheel that holds water**, allows people to roll rather than carry larger loads of water from the local well or river. It means higher productivity and better sanitation that impacts entire communities throughout Africa and Southeast Asia.

The automobile industry demonstrates another example of this trend to curb the profligate waste of the mid-and-late 20th century. Building a new car from scratch takes massive amounts of energy and materials, and recycling those materials to create new vehicles has been a multibillion-dollar industry for decades. Recently, car manufacturers have addressed the recycling issue more holistically. **Volvo and Toyota now**

make cars out of 95% recycled parts, and most significant manufacturers include steps in their design intended to make their vehicles more accessible to recycle than before.

There's the problem of producing **hybrid cars which are more pollution-intensive than the production of conventional vehicles**. The innovative incorporated technology and rarer resources call for more expensive production and disposal costs. Regular waste handling companies do not accept composite components and those that do have higher prices. Furthermore, workers who are both under-trained and poorly equipped frequently transport this toxic waste.

Our consumption of fossil fuels has led to acid rain, smog, and global warming, even in countries with advanced emission regulations. In response to those dangers, we have begun investing significant money and human resources into developing safe, **renewable sources of energy, including wind, tidal, solar, and biofuels**.

Some cities have begun fighting pollution and improving the quality of urban life by **installing community gardens** where people from the neighborhood work to produce some of the vegetables they need. Besides feeding locals, these gardens create green space to lower temperatures and improve air quality throughout the city. Most cities with such programs also give tax rebates and other benefits to companies that build or occupy **offices with lower energy footprints**. It is a worldwide movement, including cities in Germany, Spain, Australia, Brazil, Sweden, Denmark, The United States, Canada, and Iceland.

People are also working on using the gifts of the land more effectively. In Indonesia, Germany, and the United Kingdom, companies are **recovering wood from fallen trees and turning them into beautiful furniture** without having to contribute to the global deforestation epidemic. Throughout the developed world, entire movements, including the "**Freegans**" and "**Voluntary Simplicity**" choose to live while consuming as little as possible, and by reusing and recycling as much as they can. One company has built a world-spanning business out of turning recycled water bottles into fleece outerwear, recycling 80 million plastic bottles each year.

We have always tried to curb some consequences of our consumption through recycling. From our earliest history, we gave food scraps to livestock to turn food waste into more food. We smelt down used glass and metals, melt plastics, and recast paper into newly usable materials. We have even invented ways to recycle used oil into a reusable lubricant, and toxic sludges into stable and safe materials.

Striking a Balance?

"Impressive," Galacti says, "we've finished our audit of land—for now."

On the one hand, humans grow immense amounts of food from the land, while on the other we let so much go to waste. With mineral resources, we build magnificent structures and wondrous technologies, but we won't open the windows to let in the fresh air because we prefer expensive air conditioning.

"Your agile mind daily crafts planet earth so you can play, work, and eat better. Parallel to that, there is a downside to this progress, for which you are admittedly finding solutions." Galacti produces a glass of water, the line of its contents filling it exactly halfway.

The glass is both half full and half empty. The real question is: are we filling it or emptying it?

As we contemplate the question, we must consider this not just for the land itself but for the plants that grow on the ground. What happens with the land directly affects what happens with the Flora—which directly affects everything else on Earth.

5. Audit Flora

From Phytoplankton to Algae

Flora, represented by phytoplankton and algae two of the most prevalent plants on Earth. What impact is humankind having on their well-being?

"Each plant is itself a wondrous system processing air, water, and nutrients to feed all living things," Galacti lectures. "Together, they form a greater and interconnected cycle that becomes the basis for the cycle of life. Air containing oxygen, water cleansed of contaminants, and food carrying vital nutrients all come from plants.

You also rely on plants for many of your accomplishments. Natural medicines, lumber, clothing, and rubber are just a few examples. Without this web of life support, the Earth would be as deadly to man as the coldest depths of space."

He's right. **Flora forms a pivot point of life on earth**, a choke point, one of vulnerability. It is the intermediary between the air and humans, and between the land and us. It refreshes our oxygen supply and absorbs the nitrogen that makes animal life possible. **Everything is interconnected; flora is another puzzle piece that is part of the entire picture**. We're auditing the whole framework of the Universe to see where humanity stands—is the glass of peace and prosperity getting fuller or emptier?

This complex system of flora supports all life[1], including us humans. **The degree to which it remains balanced and healthy is the degree to which we can sustain human endeavors, civilization, and life.**

Is the system healthy? If not, are we working to repair it? If so, **are our actions and decisions contributing to its continued health?** Or are we pushing the system out of balance?

All Flora Small and Great

Flora on earth ranges from minute one-cell plant spores to the most significant plant witch is a tentacular mushroom covering almost 1000 hectares or the equivalent of some 1700 football fields. Each plant possesses value and faces its challenges. Let's take a closer look and see how they are faring.

Phytoplankton, small, but vital

---

1. https://theexplanation.com/dry-land-seas-and-flora-why-this-combination-on-day-3-of-creation/

Phytoplankton is a microscopic flora that inhabits every drop of the top 100 meters of every ocean on the planet. It is the largest field of plant life in the world, alone responsible for drawing as much CO_2 out of the atmosphere as all land plants combined. The various species adapt to different climates and conditions, but the effects of human pollution and global climate change are reducing all of them.

The world's population of phytoplankton has dropped by 40 percent in the past half-century, a fact with alarming implications both for the growing CO_2 imbalance and for the **ocean animals that rely on phytoplankton as their primary food source.** That list includes sea stars, shrimp, snails, many species of fish, and even whales.

Humanity has responded to this discovery with funding, research, and experimentation into what is causing the phytoplankton to die-off and what we can do about it. We understand the importance of this microflora to the ecological balance of the earth. As of this writing, restoration projects have begun testing hypotheses—but we are just at the beginning of the journey toward a solution.

All About Algae

Algae are slightly larger, but still tiny, flora that **can warn observers about the overall health of water ecosystems.** Under healthy conditions, algae provide oxygen and food for aquatic animals while growing in a controlled fashion.

Unhealthy conditions cause algae to *bloom* in a massive slick that destroys the entire local aquatic ecosystem. The slick blocks sunlight from reaching beneficial underwater plants, which can then no longer produce enough oxygen for local fish.

Even in healthy quantities, algae can become a hazard when interacting with human behavior. **Algae eat and concentrate whatever substances are in the water.** If they grow in an area that is taking in a safe amount of sulfuric acid from a nearby factory—say 1 part per million—they will concentrate that dangerous toxin within their mass. The algae can then burn or poison swimmers, pets, and livestock that swim in it. When the algae die, the dangerously concentrated contaminant sinks to the bottom of the lake to poison and kill the plants growing there.

Algae blooms happen almost exclusively when we humans impact an area via careless importation or nutrient pollution. The inadvertent introduction occurs when a species of algae is carried into a new waterway, for instance, on a boat's hull. Each waterway has its population of plants and animals, which have interacted over centuries into a working balance. When a new species of algae enters that balanced system, it can thrive due to a higher nutrient content than it is accustomed to, or from an absence of natural predators. The newly arrived algae bloom, often supplanting or destroying the original population of the waterway.

Nutrient pollution is when runoff from artificial fertilizer used in nearby farms contaminates the water. We discussed the *mixed blessing* of fertilizer in the previous section about land, but its effects on the water only illustrate how interconnected the whole system of the world is.

Algae can also be helpful, and demonstrate the innovative ways we can interact with flora to improve the world and our lives, even to help balance some of the most destructive consequences of our often shortsighted decisions.

Algae have a short life cycle, which lets scientists experiment with genetic engineering and selective breeding faster than with many other species. We have used this speedy development to **breed algae that eat waste, even hazardous waste, to clean up our mistakes.** *Microcloeus steenstrupii* is just one example of algae grown to eat oil and heavy metals contaminating water and has been **used in oil-spill cleanups worldwide.** Another alga—*c. moniliferum*—can separate strontium from nuclear accidents and trap it where it does no further harm.

Recently, French designer **Pierre Calleja developed a lamp using bioluminescent algae** as its light source, lighting urban areas as well as an electric lamp without requiring electricity. Even better, each algae lamp can absorb one ton of atmospheric carbon per year. Several other teams have developed algae that can be **used as biodiesels to reduce our dependency on fossil fuels.**

Rainforests or Monoculture?

Rainforests, one of the lungs of our planet (phytoplankton being the other) or monoculture, one of the cancers of Earth. Which shall it be?

Massive plants like trees in the rainforests or medium-sized plants like corn or a lot of other comestible food plants—each represents a piece in the interconnected puzzle of the chain of life here on Earth

Medium-sized plants

Medium-sized plants are the type of flora we most often rely on as **crops, germinate, and grow as part of a normal pollination process.** For many species, the bee population is an integral part of this cycle.

While bees collect nectar from plant flowers, pollen sticks to their legs. As the bees fly to other flowers, they pollinate the new location and allow the plant to reproduce.

For **the past five years, bee populations have declined by 25% worldwide** in mass die-offs collectively called **Colony Collapse Disorder**. Although scientists have yet to identify the cause of CCD conclusively, most evidence points to **pesticides** used in industrial farming as the most likely culprit. If the bee population continues to plummet, it destroys a necessary step in how billions of plants are fertilized each year—with the possible **results, including extinction for many plants** on which humans rely. In response, the use of organic pesticides and predator pest control has risen in the developed world to keep that chain intact.

Enormous Flora at Large

It's fair to describe the world's **forests as the "other lungs of the earth."** They recycle megatons of CO_2 into oxygen each year, supporting the air cycle for a breathable atmosphere and reducing the climate-changing CO_2 content in the air. The forests aren't as vast as the world's phytoplankton field, but still vital to keeping the systems of our planet in balance.

Beyond their role in the air cycle, the extensive **rainforests of the world produce many of our staple foods**. An incomplete list includes bananas, oranges, peppers, okra, peanuts, cashews, coffee beans, palm and coconut oil, cocoa, sugar, beans, and a variety of spices and teas.

On the positive side of the *Audit* ledger, you can also call **rainforests the "world's medicine cabinet"** because of the medicinal plants found within its varied species. As of 2014, we derive 120 prescription drugs sold worldwide directly from rainforest products to treat ailments ranging from malaria to heart disease to tuberculosis.

According to the US National Cancer Institute, **more than 2/3 of the medicines with cancer-fighting properties come from rainforest plants**. These impressive statistics don't even include manufactured drugs that based their original formula on compounds found in rainforest flora.

Despite their importance to the world environment and our survival, **deforestation is a major environmental issue**. According to UN statistics, human activity is destroying the world's forests at a rate of 5.2 million hectares per year. That's an area about the size of Costa Rica. While this rate has dropped from 8.3 million annually between 1990 and 2000, **it is still a *cancer* of the world's lungs** that inhibits their ability to foster healthy, balanced human life.

Though humankind is at the center of forest deconstruction by deforestation, many of us **humans are also at the center of preventing or even reversing deforestation**. Some examples of the most effective efforts include:

- Finding **alternatives to wood** for cooking fuel in developing nations.
- Programs of payments for reforesting land, initially, deforested for financial gain.
- National legislation creating protected forests.
- Enforcing stricter regulations on lumber and agriculture interests.
- Ecotourism programs that bring money into a region only if rainforests remain intact.
- China's "Green Wall" project, which is aggressively replanting large areas of forest razed during their early industrialization.

Enormous Opportunity

The **largest living organism in the world is a single mushroom covering 880 hectares of land in the Malheur National Forest of Oregon, USA.** It's more extensive than 24 nations. Other individual species of the same kind of mushroom can measure over 1,000 acres each. **The root structure of this massive plant is a hyper-complex network** that our scientists are using to expand our understanding of computer networks, supply chains, and even our own brain's neural net.

"I like this giant mushroom," Galacti says.

"Why is that?" I ask.

"Because I'm such a fun guy. Get it? Fungi?"

"Groan," I say out loud.

"But seriously folks," Galacti says, "**What happens to your flora happens to your atmosphere, happens to your fauna, and happens to you.** Flora is an important pivot in the life of your planet, one that cycles the resources and waste of other pieces of the puzzle so that all can survive." Every link in the chain of life counts. The fungi network is both food and responsible for food production. As such, it is a central link and another piece that must find its rightful place in the complete puzzle picture.

The Power of Biodiversity

Flora tends to thrive in an automatically balanced cycle, left without humankind's interference. Plants share air and water. Dying plants fertilize the soil for newer specimens. **Symbiotic relationships develop** between different species in a wild tangle of vibrant growth that may not be as aesthetically pleasing as a tended garden but require far less outside maintenance.

One example of this in action is the country of Brunei, located on the eastern island of Indonesia. The entire region is a megadiversity site, although the **rubber trade**, in most countries of the area, **has left its effects on local rainforests** cutting into that diversity and limiting it significantly.

Brunei, by contrast, was an oil-producing nation from its inception, which meant they never harvested their old-growth timber the way other parts of the region did. **If left to flourish unmolested, their rainforests reach heights of nearly 200 feet and are home to vast arrays of land and water wildlife**. These species work together in an intricate web that depends on the healthy balance of the flora.

The counterexample is the modern agricultural practice of monoculture[1]: raising only one crop or product without using the land for other purposes. A **cornfield** in a modern Western farm is home only to corn, fertilized optimally for corn, and considers all other plants to be weeds. Monocultural fields are less expensive to plant and harvest than diverse areas but have several disadvantages.

The plants grown there – being of a single species or narrow range of species – are **more vulnerable to pests and disease**. The arrangement makes inefficient use of resources because the same patch of land could grow and support more than one crop, and **fails to provide a rich habitat for other flora and fauna**.

As with our efforts against deforestation, we have produced some ingenious efforts to **increase and encourage biodiversity** to curb the trend toward monoculture farming.

- Government and multinational efforts and regulations to preserve species and encourage biodiverse agriculture.
- Agriculture associations are making efforts to support and

---

1. https://theexplanation.com/agricultural-land-its-real-green-long-term-value/

make a case for returning to biodiverse farming models.

- The general public is becoming more aware of the quality and provenance of their groceries. They're looking for fresher produce and a more local and sustainable food supply chain.

"So much of man's relationship with flora is based on food," Galacti notes. "Flora feeds you directly, or through your eating the animals that eat it. I wonder why so often it seems that you value money over plants? Don't you use much of the money to buy food?"

Our species has been agrarian since its inception. Has our [2]**relationship with food moved from a process based on growing nutrition to a method of increasing profits?** Are we using fertilizer instead of natural nutrients to grow food as quickly as possible to provide the most substantial, most profitable yields—quantity over quality?

Is pesticide application to produce as much of the harvest as possible a short-term solution? What is the **food industry's responsibility in flora poisoning**—depleting its nutritional value and, at the same time, throwing land and human health out of balance?

It is the answer to such questions that tell us if the glass of health and prosperity is getting fuller or emptier.

---

2. https://theexplanation.com/light-to-dark-adam-eves-brutal-switch-from-open-to-closed-minds/

GMO – Way to Feed the World?

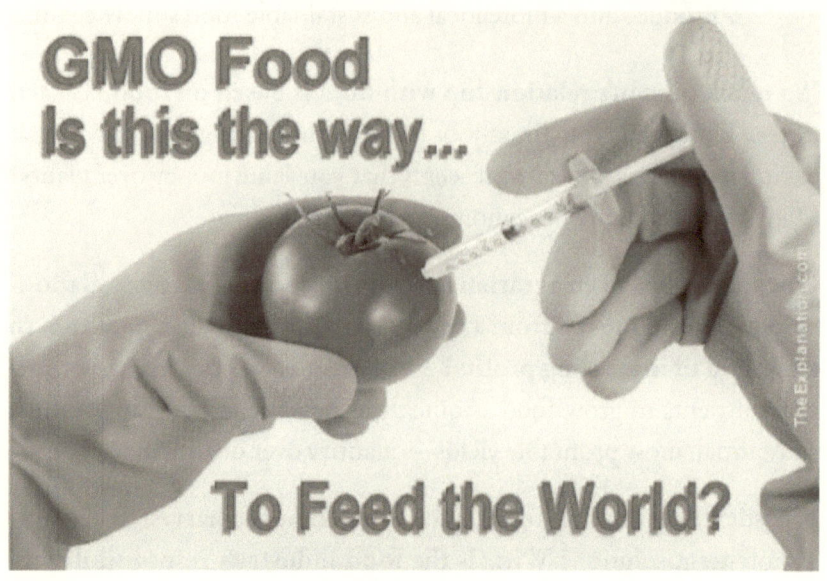

GMO - Genetically Modified Organism. Intervening in the food we eat, at the gene level. Pros and Cons

Giving Flora a Helping Human Hand

The debate over genetically modified foods (GMO) has raged over the past decade. Some nations have embraced them. Some have banned them outright. Some people are violently opposed, while others are firmly in favor. Very few have no opinion at all.

On the plus side, genetically modified plants let us breed or design them for human-positive qualities. A genetically modified plant can produce more food faster, resist pests without relying on poisonous sprays, survive in more diverse climates, and repel more diseases. Humankind has a **millennia-old tradition of crossbreeding plant species** for these exact characteristics and has only recently begun tinkering at the direct genetic level.

We have genetically engineered every one of our staple food crops for thousands of years. This process started with simple selection: weeding out less desirable strains while planting the more suitable. Cross-pollination and hybridization came next, with a variety of plants with the most advantageous mutations. Up to this point, where only natural reproductive methods come into play, species maintain their integrity, and those that can't are either sterile or die out.

Then there's the **next level where human intervention is necessary**: Inducing **mutation via chemicals or radiation and direct genetic manipulation**; this opened the door to the practice of producing real genetically modified flora.

From the first marketing of **DNA modified tomatoes, in 1994**, to delay their ripening, this genetic tinkering has been castigated by opponents of GMOs who cite a variety of risks and disadvantages:

- Some fear that GMO crops could be **increasing allergenic properties**, explaining the rise in food allergies.
- There is widespread concern, with some statistical support, that some GMO foods **contain carcinogenic compounds**.
- Creating plants **immune to bacteria** encourages bacteria to breed more robust strains, which some believe will ultimately result in more antibiotic-resistant strains. Similarly, herbicidal and pesticidal crops might give rise to *super-weeds* and *super-pests*.
- Many GMO crops **underperform traditional plants** in terms of **nutritional content** and taste.

At the nexus of the GMO and industrialization debate is the fact that **GMO crops are part of intellectual copyright law.** It creates situations where a farmer who uses GMO seeds must **pay for seed every season**, as opposed to natural plants where you could use the seeds produced in one planting for the next round.

It is putting **small farmers**, especially in more impoverished areas of Asia and Africa, in jeopardy as they **cannot afford to buy seed for the next growing season.** Agriculture employs 40% of the world's population and even up to 75% in poorer nations. **GMOs are throwing people off their land** with devastating consequences.

GMO supporters often point out that most of the **objections to GMOs are about what *could happen*** as opposed to what has been demonstrated. They counter with some of the possibilities for GMO crops as our mastery of this technology continues to improve.

We could develop crops to **survive in deserts and high-salinity areas**, reclaiming land lost to earlier mistakes. Even deeper into science fiction, there are plants designed to be edible vaccines or treatments for illness. We are also now working to develop plants to treat cholera, AIDS, and chronic diarrhea.

The debate will go on regarding the pros and cons. Is our proverbial glass of healthy, vibrant, and bio-diverse flora getting fuller or emptier?

The Creative Destruction of Slash-and-Burn Farming

Slash-and-burn is a method of farming by which you gain arable land by destroying the surrounding rainforest. The process begins with cutting down vegetation in an area, sometimes via clearcutting, felling everything in sight, and in other cases leaving only food-bearing trees alive. You then let the downed vegetation dry until just before the rainiest part of the season; then, you burn the tinder-dry leaves and twigs.

This burning provides several **immediate benefits**. The smoke drives away or **kills pests** and vermin that would otherwise prey on the crop. The **ashes are an excellent fertilizer** for the first few growing seasons, after which you abandon the plot to slash and burn another piece of rainforest.

In **sustainable slash-and-burn farms**, you cycle through several parcels of land over the decades. Once vegetation on a burned plot has grown to a point, it can produce enough ash; you return to the previously slashed-and-burned area instead of cutting down more rainforest. However, this sustainable cycle is not always adopted.

In regions where economies are tight, and an autocratic government controls the land, farmers continue slashing and burning into the rainforest. At the same time, previously cleared plots are abandoned or converted to urban areas. Even with a sustainable approach, the process **contributes to deforestation, accelerated erosion, and loss of biodiversity**.

The **QSMAS** (Quesungual Slash and Mulch Agroforestry System) is a variation of slash-and-burn applied by researchers in South and Central America. It offers a compromise between the economic benefits of slash-and-burn and a balanced approach. Also called *slash-and-mulch*, you begin the process with a developed tract of secondary forest in which you sow pioneer crops like sorghum or beans that thrive in such an environment.

Once seedlings appear, you practice selective slashing of low-value shrubs and prune any food-bearing trees. This slash creates a layer of decomposing plant matter that mulches to fertilize new plants. The crops grow among high-value timber and fruit trees left alive. After the first growing season, your plot is ready for higher-yield, more fragile crops like maize.

The QSMAS program[1] alone has produced food security for thousands of small-scale farmers in developing nations, increased the average value of maize and bean production by 81%, and recovered local biodiversity in approximately 60,000 hectares of secondary forest. That's a land area about the size of Norway.

Some **other creative farming solutions** we have adopted include vertical farming in urban areas, the organic food movement, and locavorism – all **moves to re-integrate, producing food with those who consume it.**

Planting Roots, But How Deep?

Galacti gestures at the plants nearby, indicating without a word that we should **consider the complex system of plant life throughout the world**. "A healthy system is sustainable and balanced, needing little or no outside interference to continue thriving.

I ask you: **is this system healthy? Will it continue to provide for humankind's needs** in the time of your children and grandchildren? Is it producing plentiful, nutritious, tasty food as it did for you in your youth? **Or is the world heading for a time of less abundance**, diversity, and nutrition available in its food basket?"

What's the answer? Are we tipping the balance to a fuller or an emptier healthy pantry?

---

1. http://blog.ciat.cgiar.org/the-quesungual-agroforestry-system-takes-root-in-nicaragua/

6. Audit Fauna

Fauna as gods and Livestock

The state of fauna: Revered on one side, raised as livestock on the other. How do humans respect animals?

Another wave of Galacti's hand and we find ourselves **standing in an animal park**. Plants still surround us: as we've seen, they're necessary for any animals to survive! But it's the creatures great and small that command our attention – birds, beasts, fish in ponds, whales in enormous pools. I am struck by the variety and majesty of all the Earth's creatures.

"When we last looked at the fauna of the earth," Galacti tells us, "we said they each had skills and roles that helped them survive in the competitive, often brutal, world of fauna. We identified communicators like bees and dolphins, organizers like ants, navigators like the carrier pigeon, climbers like monkeys, swimmers like beavers, tool-makers like otters, and home-builders like badgers. Within their areas of specialization, **animals have physical abilities and instinctual skills that make them the world-leading best at what they do.**"

I remember thinking back to Chapter Six of *Inventory of the Universe*[1] and the **amazing capabilities of the animals** with which we share the Earth.

"But man has divided them into other categories, according to your relationship with each. This categorization has powerfully affected how well an animal lives, and how likely a species is to survive into the next century."

"I hadn't thought of it that way," I admit. But he's right.

Animals as Elders

Early religions often held many animals equal to or higher than humans. We would imagine they had human souls and developed animistic and totemistic beliefs around respecting or warring with those souls (depending on the individual culture). Some of our ancient societies **elevated animals to the status of gods.** The ancient **Egyptians** worshiped cats and crocodiles, while **Native Americans** revered the spirits of the Bear, Raven, and others. Even in cultures that placed less importance on the animals around us, we lived in balance with the fauna of the Earth. Humans had not yet developed the technology to do anything else.

As man modernized, that balance changed. **Humans have become the dominant life form on the planet, and our decisions affect the lives of every creature with which we share it.** Those effects rely on our relationship with each kind of animal:

---

1. http://theexplanation.com/animal-abilities-animal-communication/

- Those we consider *possessions*, for which we feel a sort of paternal responsibility or mutually beneficial symbiosis.
- Nuisances and threats, which we work tirelessly to reduce or eradicate.
- Some we rarely notice. These animals may have the saddest fate of all.

In this final part of *Audit of the Universe*, we join Galacti for an in-depth look at animals in these relationships. We examine how humans have changed their lot for good or ill.

For better or worse, we are the most powerful form of life on Earth.

"Better for humans, certainly. How has it worked out for the animals around them?" Galacti suggests.

"Wait for it," I say. "We'll see."

Because of this position, we have, for thousands of years, considered some kinds of animals as belonging to us. Depending on the animal in question, this has worked out better or worse for them.

Livestock

Traditionally, we lived with cattle in a balanced symbiosis. **Family farmers and ranchers raised their animals carefully**, fed them appropriately, and slaughtered them for food at a pace that kept up with reproduction. We understood that killing our food animals faster than that would mean less food in the years to come. This relationship allowed the animals, as a species, to survive more readily than in the wild – though the final fate of any individual animal could be considered grim. The arrangement also helped us, since we got nutrition from each animal without having to expend calories or risk injuries on the hunt.

Modern industrial farming stands in sharp and ugly contrast. Animals are born and die in small pens, often lacking room even to turn around. They get packed together by the thousands in spaces that breed disease and house hosts of parasites. **Health can be neglected** since the *acceptable losses* of a few hundred individuals per growing season costs less than health care for thousands.

Most industrial raised livestock are injected with **massive doses of antibiotics**, and some nations still permit hormone treatments to make the animals grow faster and fatter. Though research is still ongoing, there are strong indications that residue from both remains in the meat and **harms the health of those who eat it**. What is more certain is that such treatment **degrades the quality of life for all animals** born, grown, and slaughtered within the industrial livestock system.

As with most situations where we are involved, **industrial farming demonstrates our dual nature.** On one side, you see inhumane and potentially harmful methods adopted because they foster easy profits. On the other, you have individuals like Dr. Temple Grandin.

Dr. Grandin is a researcher in human and animal behavior and has designed several stockyards, corrals, races, chutes, and loading ramps specifically built to **give food animals better-living conditions and a more humane slaughter**. For example, she designed a curved cattle chute that takes advantage of the natural movement of cows. Cattle moving through this chute experience less distress and require less prodding from handlers while walking through the chute. She teaches at Colorado State University in Fort Collins, Colorado, to **lead research in sustainable, humane relationships between livestock and we humans** who need them.

She is but one example of a **general movement toward a more balanced relationship with our food animals**. A variety of grassroots movements throughout the industrial world have opted for the humane treatment of livestock. Farmers and ranchers choose to keep their animals in cage-free conditions and let them roam large fields and pastures while eating natural healthy foods.

Animals in such situations are **less subject to disease and parasites**, meaning the massive injections of antibiotics aren't necessary. In support of this more humane approach, consumers – both private customers and restaurant supply buyers – voluntarily spend between 20 and 150% more on meat from these sources.

Endangered Species & Humans

Endangered species of animals hold a special place in human hearts. We love animals, but never before have we been in danger of losing so many species.

Forbidden animals

Endangered species of animals[1] has caused humanity to take a step back and look at what we're doing with the animal population. One aspect of considering something a possession is giving oneself permission to damage or break it. **Animal testing runs the gamut from psychological torture to actual vivisection** to intentionally giving an animal cancer. In some cases, this treatment is arguably a necessary step in improv-

1. https://www.worldwildlife.org/species/directory?direction=desc&sort=extinction_status

ing human quality and quantity of life – as in testing drugs and medical procedures on animals before approving them for human trials. In others, cruelty is part of manufacturing a luxury like snack foods or cosmetics.

But not everybody supports this kind of treatment for animals. PETA (People for the Ethical Treatment of Animals), the Animal Welfare Enforcement Agency in Britain, and China's Voice4Animals are just three organizations – with a total membership exceeding one million – that **organize protests and pursue legal channels to reduce and eliminate needless animal cruelty**. Three examples of the auspicious influence of such organizations are the cases of ivory, whaling, and fur.

- We've hunted elephants, rhinoceros, walrus, and dozens of other species with **tusks or ivory horns for centuries,** a lot of which are endangered species. The rest of their bodies were habitually left abandoned after recuperating the high-value ivory. Throughout the mid-20th-century, a combination of public opinion and legal change reduced the ivory trade to a trickle of illegally poached specimens. Unfortunately, as of Nov. 2017, Trump has lifted the US ban on elephant trophy hunting.
- **Fancy furs** from animals like beaver, ermine and mink, once drove entire economies and reduced species like the American buffalo to near-extinction. Like ivory-bearing species, these animals were rarely eaten, and the bodies were wasted after their skins were removed. During the late 20th century, protests staged in significant shopping areas turned public opinion against wearing such coats. Though few legal restrictions are in place against producing fur, the demand has dropped sufficiently to reduce production by half between the 1960s and 2010.

- Throughout the 15th through 19th centuries, **whales** were hunted for their meat and the blubber, which produced clean-burning lamp oil. Modern whaling techniques made the hunt exponentially easier for humans, and correspondingly hard on whale populations. Some endangered species neared extinction before groups – most notably Greenpeace – campaigned on behalf of these highly advanced forms of animals. As of 2014, whaling is only legal in Japan, Norway, and Iceland.

This video of a starving polar bear[2] is a heart wrencher.

Animal favorites of Humans

Perhaps the most fortunate of animals are those for whom we have developed real affection. Man views our pets as, if not our children, favored younger siblings for which we feel both love and responsibility. These animals include those we keep as pets and those we have decided to protect because of their beauty, exoticness, or rarity.

Pets are often cared for as if they were children: and Americans alone spend a total of $61.4 billion on their pets annually. Different countries and regions consider different animals appropriate for keeping as pets. In China, cats are in luck, while Americans prefer dogs. Japanese keep birds and crickets. Inuit Eskimos of Canada might care for a fox, seal, or even bear cub. We don't always regard working animals like oxen and horses with the same affection as pets, but we usually treat them nearly as well because we rely on them to help accomplish our work.

Another class of animals we care for are those who have adapted to live in the human sphere. We don't view them as possessions *per se*, but we create and possess the environment in which they have become

---

comfortable. Animals like rats and pigeons thrive in human cities, and some animals, including raccoons, opossums, monkeys, and coyotes have adapted to urban environments in the past several decades. This relationship works out to their advantage, even if we aren't willing partners in the exchange.

Exotic animals, when we're not hunting them, sometimes land in this category as well. In most cases, this is after the animal has reached the brink of extinction. We overfish, overhunt, or destroy their environment through our industry and expansion. Once an exotic animal's endangerment alerts public attention, international and grassroots movements sometimes champion their cause.

Since 1973, 180 nations have ratified the Convention on International Trade in Endangered Species treaty, which aims at protecting over 35,000 species of animals and plants. The protected fauna include the red panda, chimpanzee, Asiatic lion, an Asian elephant among many others—all examples of creatures which have become valued by humanity because of their exotic and endangered status.

In the United States, the Endangered Species Act has helped 93 species recover from endangered status to establish healthy populations. Although this is good news, realize that it's just 1 percent of the species protected by the Act, and the recovery time is typically 20-25 years.

Other valid acts and treaties include the **Migratory Bird Treaty** between Canada and Great Britain of 1916, the Antarctic Treaty of 1959, which defined rules for studying and preserving the area around that continent, and the 1989 African Elephant Conservation Act.

Humans don't always make the right decisions[3], but as you can see, they can come around to aid those animals who need help. Case in point, the first-ever birth at the Beauval Zoo, South West of Paris, of a baby Panda in August 2017, which was officially named *Yuan Meng*, meaning *the realization of a wish* by Brigitte Macron, wife of the French President. It is a joint venture between France and China to revive the Panda population[4], another endangered species, and is the result of real efforts towards that goal.

Nuisances and Threats

We have not always been the top predator in the global environment, and even in modern times, **animals kill several hundred people each year**. When not attacking us directly, predators can harm or kill the animals we have chosen to protect. These factors lead us to view some animals as enemies to be destroyed, and not as possessions to exploit or friends in our care.

For centuries, this relationship was like a well-matched boxing bout. Two opponents – the tiger on one side and us on the other, for example. We stalked and hunted one another, maybe not fair, but it wasn't one-sided. Since the industrial revolution, this conflict has grown more and more to resemble a fight between a schoolyard bully and his skinny victim. **Our tools of hunting and war have driven many top predators to extinction**, and the survivors into a few remaining pockets of deep wilderness.

We don't view vermin and pests as the threats that predators are, but humans hunt and kill them with the same efficiency. Eliminating rodents, insects, and similar creatures is an 11-billion-dollar industry in

---

3. https://theexplanation.com/light-to-dark-adam-eves-brutal-switch-from-open-to-closed-minds/

4. https://youtu.be/CLH6q-fx3pA

the US alone. Even before the process became industrialized, individual people have made a living, trapping rats since we started living in cities. These vermin are often disease vectors, trapping, and killing them is likely a necessary cost of what some might consider the advantages of urbanizing humanity.

Bacteria is another form of fauna humans have viewed as a threat since we discovered them in the 19th century. We have acted to counter this threat with antibiotics, antiseptics, and vaccines. This campaign has improved our lifespans and quality of life. Still, it has also forced bacteria to reorganize and evolve, creating super-resistant bacteria that are immune to many of our antibiotics. **Cases like this are essential studies in our *Audit of the Universe*** since unintended consequences play a significant role in our effect on the Universe. The Coronavirus pandemic of 2020 is witness to the boomerang effect fauna can have on humans.

Balance of Animals Still True

Trophy Animals

At the intersection of animals, we view as possessions, and those we perceive as threats are the animals we hunt for trophies. We kill approximately 100 million animals each year[1] as hunting trophies, including threatened and endangered species like lions, polar bears, and rhinoceros.

---

1. http://www.da4a.org/sport.htm

Although this seems barbaric to some, there is strong evidence that **sport hunting plays an essential role in maintaining a balanced ecosystem**. There's even more evidence that hunters and fishers are among the most vocal supporters of environmental conservation. Much like the original farmers and herdsmen cared for animals so their supply of meat wouldn't end, hunters and fishers understand that damage to the environment threatens their ability to hunt and fish. They go to great lengths to protect the environment their fish and game call home and to preserve it so they can share their pastime with their children.

Poachers are an exception to this hunters-as-stewards-of-animals situation. These parasitic humans kill or capture exotic animals for profit, violating national and international laws as they do so. Since they are already breaking the law, poachers pay little attention to laws about animal cruelty. United Nations research reports that illegal hunting and trapping of exotic animals could eliminate the wild populations of several species of rhino, gorilla, and tiger by 2025.

The Forgotten Animals

The least healthy relationship with us likely belongs to those **animals with whom we have no affiliation**. According to figures from the Center for Biological Diversity, we have endangered thousands of species of amphibians, birds, invertebrates, and reptiles **primarily because we are destroying or fundamentally altering their habitats**. As we require more and more land for living, farming, mining, and even waste disposal, we take that land from areas that were once safe havens for animals.

This kind of destruction also happens when **humans attempt to eliminate an *enemy* animal** by aggressively killing the top-level predator. It upsets the local ecosystem and can endanger species we never even knew existed. For example, killing all of the wolves in an area allows the deer population to rise. Those deer eat more local plants than is sustainable, leading herbivores in the area to die of starvation. That same over-consumption of plant leaves causes less shade on the nearby river, harming that ecosystem as the water temperature rises.

In the ocean off Japan, **swarms of 450-pound jellyfish appear in populations of hundreds and thousands.** These giants – called Nomura's Jellyfish – have existed for eons, but only began appearing in such large numbers recently. Like the algae blooms we discussed, this is a **sign of an imbalance in the ecosystem** these creatures inhabit. Scientists are still investigating the causes, but a betting man would put his money on the unanticipated, unintentional result of something we did.

Invaders from Inner Space

"Fauna creates a system, and **like all systems, it must be in balance to properly work**," Galacti says.

"True. If a car had tires of four different sizes, it wouldn't go very far."

"Nor would the ride be very comfortable," he replies. "**Fauna in nature lives in a state of competition.** In ecosystems left to themselves, the **animals form a balance where no species becomes dominant.** If you transplant a new species into such a system, one with no natural predators or which thrives especially well in its new environment, it can overrun the area to the detriment of other species and of itself."

The image of a brown tree snake forms in my mind. **Humans introduced this snake to Guam and other Pacific Islands to curb the growing rat population.** That plan worked, but we forgot to take into account one small fact: snakes find birds delicious. The island avians, having grown and developed in an environment devoid of snakes, had no defense. Many species of birds are now extinct or facing extinction because of brown snake predation.

Other species with similar, if not as drastic, invasive effects include zebra mussels, mongoose, and raccoons. King crabs are wiping out fish in certain areas, and Asian carp are threatening the Great Lakes[2] after taking over parts of the Mississippi and its tributaries. In all cases, we humans brought the unbalancing newcomer to the party, most often for good reasons – but we did not anticipate the potential consequences as visible in this video[3].

Until the past few decades, we allowed this kind of species importation without any oversight or restriction. Since the 1970s, though, we have become more aware of the destructive potential of invasive species. As of this writing, **over 100 countries have signed biodiversity laws aimed to restore or maintain proper balance among fauna and flora species**.

The Human Balancing Act

Galacti gestures to all the animals in the park around us. As I look at each one, my mind fills with visual impressions of **how that species has fared at the hand of humans**, the dominant form of life on land.

"When we were with the plants," he says, "we saw how humanity's relationship with the earth moved you further and further from your connection with the world of plants. Much the same has happened to your relationship with animals. As your daily lives have drawn away from the animals, you have noticed less the impact your decisions have on those you share the earth with."

Man is the highest form of life on Earth, but we live alongside and share our planet with animals and plants. Balance in our relationship is essential for their as well as our health and well-being. We must ask ourselves: based on the evidence scrolling through our mind's eye, **have the**

---

2. https://www.theguardian.com/world/2017/jun/24/asian-carp-great-lakes-michigan-illinois

3. https://youtu.be/YnZp1jtOhR0

last 10 to 20 years been to the benefit of the animals, and even to ourselves? What trajectory are we following concerning our relationship with nature and animals in particular?

7. Audit Human Life

Human Life is the Highest Level on Earth

Human life is superior to all other life forms on Earth. Humankind is the number one factor that affects our planet. What is human life?

Expanding the comprehension of human life is the subject of this chapter. It transitions us into the last three sections of *Audit of the Universe* and the five sections of *Audit of Humankind* that focus on humanity. It so happens that humankind is unique in ways I'll elaborate in these chapters. Remember, the focus of our quest is: How to establish peace and prosperity on Earth. Humankind, ranking as the highest form of life, has a definite responsibility in finding this pathway.

Inventory of the Universe delved into the mechanics of human life: Genes[1], DNA[2], stem cells[3], reproduction, chronobiology[4], and many other aspects of how humans are composed. *Audit of the Universe* is a summary of where humankind is in this search for harmony on our planet. But *Audit* would not be complete without a deeper understanding of humanity: **Men, women, children, families, relationships. How do individuals, males, and females, groups like communities, races, and nations function and think?** These upcoming chapters here, and in *Audit of Humankind*, the third book in *The Explanation* series, delve into the difficulties of humankind.

We are going to start by defining what human life is. Down through the ages, men have given their best efforts to try to explain social life. You'll recognize the names of some significant philosophers who describe humankind.

The Philosophies of Humans on what is Human Life? Just who are we?

Plato wrote about how we humans have created communities as a way of reinforcing the power of our reason and communication. With animals, a struggle for power or disagreement always goes to the physically strongest in the herd. Human civilization, by contrast, provides a way for **the smartest or most socially adept person** to lead.

We don't compete with animals on a physical level; our society has simultaneously supported and been supported by the advanced cognitive power that differentiates us from the animals.

---

1. http://theexplanation.com/mouse-has-more-genes-than-a-human-being-that-should-humble-us/

2. http://theexplanation.com/nucleotides-and-dna-millions-of-parts-assembled-perfectly/

3. http://theexplanation.com/stem-cells-differentiation-core-of-your-body-s-regeneration-process/

4. http://theexplanation.com/pollination-chronobiology-flora-how-it-works/

Aristotle pointed to **communication as the factor that defines us.** Although some animals are capable of simple communication, only human language captures abstract concepts. A bird can indicate the location of food, but only we can communicate what a space looked like before the food arrived, or describe a plan for growing more food tomorrow. In his discussion of this vital difference, Aristotle also indicated another uniquely human quality – **our ability to discuss and internalize moral codes. Morals and ethics are inherently abstract concepts,** and only a being who can **think and communicate in the abstract** can be a moral or ethical creature.

"Or *im*moral and *un*ethical," Galacti points out. Reminding us that *Audit of the Universe* is about the state of Earth today, with each of us having to evaluate whether the glass of peace and prosperity is getting fuller or emptier—more or less moral and ethical.

Rene Descartes, famous for saying "I think; therefore I am," added the observation that **true cognition is only possible through abstract language.** The conversations we have with ourselves, the internal thoughts which so define our lives as humans, are only possible with the **abstract words and ideas unique to humankind.** He said, "Animals are machines without souls. Lacking consciousness, they are incapable of thought. They follow instinct."

Kant agrees, writing that of all creatures on earth, only we are not servants to instinct. Animals are aware of their current circumstance, but we humans can imagine changes to our situations. **This imagination, unique to our human life, is the foundation for everything we have accomplished.** Kant also expanded on the discussion Aristotle started, pointing out that **only when free of instinct can we be capable of forming morality.** Any individual human among us has the freedom to follow or not follow ethics and morals, while a hungry predator must kill. It lacks the ability of conscious choice we take for granted.

Rousseau built on this conversation by adding **the concept of "perfectability."** By this, he didn't mean that we are perfect, or even that we can become perfect. Instead, he identified **humans as the only beings on earth that can learn and improve upon themselves.** Lions 10,000 years ago lived and behaved as lions do today. Sharks have been sharks for millions of years. But we, and we alone, can change and transform as individuals and as a species. Animals obey their instinct, says Rousseau, and thus neither gain nor lose anything from generation to generation. **We use intellect, experimentation, and imagination to learn, grow, change,** and alter our environment through construction, innovation, and invention.

In the late 19th century, **Bergson** identified **inventiveness** as another characteristic unique to us. Some animals create tools, such as a monkey thrusting a stick into a termite mound to gather a tasty snack, but even the most advanced animal uses but one or two tools and even then uses only simple, found objects. They don't manufacture tools. **Humankind uses and fabricates a wide variety of devices,** and also invents tools for the express purpose of building other tools; this is the flip side of Rousseau's perfectability. We have not only the capacity to change ourselves but also the capacity to improve our environment.

"As an aside, consider that how we use that inventiveness for good or ill can be inconsistent," I admit. Galacti raises one eyebrow in arch agreement.

During the 20th century, **Heidegger** discussed existence as a concept and defined us as **the only creatures on earth that exist.** He argued that animals were conscious and aware, but **actual existence requires three abilities**:

- The ability to **see far-reaching possibilities**
- The ability to **analyze potential consequences**

- The ability to **make decisions based on those possibilities and analysis**

Of all species on earth, only we have demonstrated even one of those three definitions.

"Over the centuries," Galacti summarizes, "some of humanity's most intelligent minds have discussed, debated and considered the differences between man and animals. They have expressed a variety of viewpoints that differentiates the two, but are united overall in the opinion that **humankind is somehow *more than* the animals.**"

"But how?" I ask.

"In trying to identify qualities that make humans, human, philosophers identified several traits: civilization, language, abstract thought, morals, ethics, perfectability, technology, analysis. Put together; they represent different **facets of the same human gem: cognitive capacity beyond the physical mechanics of the brain.** All animals have brains and are capable of incredible prowesses, but only humans possess a *mind*."

Museums Reveal the Essence of Being Human

Being human and the definition of human life have been enigmas from time immemorial. Can we give a definitive answer to this dilemma? Yes.

I've been thinking and working on *The Explanation* series for a good part of my life. Some fifteen years ago, I visited the evolution gallery of the British Museum[1]. I wanted to see how various classes of scientists defined *human*. What is it that sets us apart and at the pinnacle of living creatures on Earth?

First, for clarity sake, I want to elaborate **what humankind has in common with animal kind:**

---

1. http://www.nhm.ac.uk/visit/galleries-and-museum-map/human-evolution.html

- Both have **physical bodies and skeletons** made of bony material. We know that some animals do not have a skeletal structure like jellyfish. There are exceptions to all these points.
- Both have a **blood circulation system** to feed the cells in their bodies.
- Both have an **oxygen circulation system** to burn the food (sugars, fatty acids) and supply the energy to their cells.

Both **humans and animals have life,** and if we break certain parts of the physical body, both die. If we cut off blood circulation, both die. If we cut off oxygen circulation, both die. In these three areas of life—physical body, blood, oxygen—although the functioning of these significant life systems can be extremely different—fish breathe oxygen underwater, humans can not—**both animals and humans are comparable**.

Now let's see the **focus of the British Museum** along with the Smithsonian, the Louvre, and the Cairo Museum. They are probably the most renowned in the world and should be able to enlighten us in our quest to pierce the mystery of what being human is all about.

There are **many exhibits of the** physical specifics of humankind.[2] Here is a very brief summary of their traits:

- **bipedalism** - The ability to stand upright and walk for lengthy periods. Our human skeleton is adapted from its central cranial base attachment to the spine. Then, down to its pelvis and the feet via the strength of the femur and articulation of the knees. From head to toe, humans stand upright.
- **Big brains** - Humans do not have the biggest brain (human brain about 1.5 kg). Sperm whales weigh in at 8 kg. But humans have the biggest brain compared to their body weight.

---

2. http://www.nhm.ac.uk/discover/how-we-became-human.html

Anthropologists admit, 'what caused this drastic increase in size is unclear[3]' but believe this human trait allowed humankind to progress and develop more sophisticated hunting tools and strategies, social structures and eventually language.

I don't want to dwell on these physical traits, but the British Museum exposes three other differences identifying humans:

- **Similar sized sexes** – Male animals were much bigger and equipped with canines to fight for females.
- **Childhood** - The ability of humans to take care of their young after weaning.
- **A precision hand-grip** - Manual dexterity to firmly grasp a small object between our thumb and the tips of our fingers.

All of these five physical traits contribute to set humans apart and make our species unique.

But let's take it a step further. If these human skeletal characteristics are important of and by themselves, what is more vital, is what they allow us to accomplish. **Bipedalism** enables us to practice sports of all types. **Brains** allow us to do research and mathematical calculations. **Similar sized sexes** enable men and women to cooperate more rationally. **Childhood** is not a *skeletal trait*, and I'm not sure why the British Museum includes it in the list. This trait is primary for humans, and I will return to it at length in chapter 3 of *Audit of Humankind* about how humans socialize. **Precision-grip** permits us to manipulate our environment and tools in umpteen ways.

---

3. http://www.nhm.ac.uk/discover/how-we-became-human.html

I realize what the vocation of the **British Museum is: focusing on the physical traits of human beings,** the morphology of skeletal remains, as revealed by archaeology, anthropology, and like sciences. However, in so doing, we reduce and even limit comprehension of humankind to just a physical level. But this emphasis **clouds the essential.**

The definition of what **being human involves deserves a much more profound analysis** rather than just scrutinizing material parts of dead bodies. Human life is vastly more than that. As important as these physical abilities are, what is capital is what they enable humans to undertake and what humankind has accomplished with them.

Skeletal traits are useless without *something* **to supervise and administer them,** so the physical body knows how to perform. In the last chapter, philosophers indicated the characteristics of humans. What being human is all about: civilization, language, abstract thought, morals, ethics, perfectability, technology, analysis.

The physical body alone can not produce any of these traits. **These are cognitive attributes.** Some people, most people, would **attribute these characteristics to the brain.** Animals have brains, but they have none of these philosophers differentiating attributes. People would say that animals have lower levels of some of these characteristics. Yes, much lower levels. Some would add that the human brain is *more developed* than the animal brain. Yes, vastly more advanced. Then we can add *instinct* **into the equation**—but there again, there remains a vast chasm between animal instinct and the capacity of being human.

I submit to you that **to bridge this massive chasm,** separating animals from **humankind, we need the** *cognitive capacity of humans.* The dictionary defines cognition[4]: relating to the **mental** processes of percep-

---

4. http://www.dictionary.com/browse/cognitive

tion, memory, judgment, and reasoning, as contrasted with emotional and volitional processes. **The seat of this mental capacity refers to the *mind*.**

Museums Reveal what Being Human is

Let's stay with the theme of museums and reveal what being human is. In *Inventory of the Universe* chapter 10[5], I compared humankind and animal kind. In *Audit of Humankind,* we will take it to a far superior level. **Other than bodily and skeletal comparisons, there is absolutely no similitude whatsoever between humans and animals.** The gulf is so great; it is insurmountable.

France, where I live, is the country of museums. **No other country has a density of museums as France does.** There are about 1250 officially recognized throughout the country. But to this must be added thousands of municipal and local museums. They fall into multiple categories.

As you read through this list, I'd like you to think of one point: **Being Human is ALL these subjects. Being Human is ALL these activities. Being Human is all this creation. Being Human is all these accomplishments.** Human Life is ALL the stories told by these museums.

Being Human is a never-ending story in itself.

---

5. http://theexplanation.com/category/animal-man-comparison/

A	H	P, R
Artillery museum	Hair museum	Palace museum
Aviation museum	Hall of Memory	Postal museum
C	Heritage centre	Prefectural mus.
Cabinet curiosities	**I**	Private museum
Ceramics museum	Imaginarium	Public museum
Children's Mus.	Interpretation	Regimental mus.
Collection (art)	**J**	Rural history
Community	Jewish museum	**S**
Computer	**L**	Science fiction
D	Lapidarium	Science museum
Dime museum	Living museum	Sex museum
E	Local museum	Ship museum
Ecomuseum	**M**	**T**
Economuseum	Maritime museum	Technology
Ethnographic mus	Migration	Textile museum
F	Mobile museum	Torture museum
Farm museum	Musaeum	Toy museum
Fashion museum	**N**	Transport mus.
Folk museum	National History	Design museum
Food museum	Natural history	**U, V, W**
G	**O**	University mus.
Geology museum	Open-air museum	Virtual museum
Green museum		Wax museum

There's **something innate about being human that places hu-mankind at a higher level**.

It's the **capacity of the human brain and mind.** Only humankind, of all the creatures on earth, are **dreamers and thinkers and poets as witnessed by all the museum collections. Humankind lives light years beyond its skeletal and biological existence and concerns itself with a mental, civil, cultural even spiritual, life.** It is the reason why humans rule planet Earth as the loftiest expression of life.

Did you notice the *Imaginarium* in the list of museums? Being human, each person who has walked the face of this Earth is **innately equipped with imagination.** The ability to come up with new concepts about every imaginable and even unimaginable subject—like creating a museum dedicated to *imagination*! **That's the epitome of mind, the characteristic of being human.**

Wow, it makes you stop and think.

Humans. Material and Immaterial?

Each human being is composed of physical elements like Carbon and Oxygen, but are there others that are not in the Periodic Table of Elements?

We're answering the very philosophical and elusive question: What is a Human Being? We've given renowned philosophers the chance to provide their insights[1] about human life: Civilization, language, abstract thought, morals, ethics, perfectability, technology, and analysis.

We've given the British Museum the chance to tell us about humankind's skeletal differences[2]: Bipedalism, big brains, similar-sized sexes, childhood, and a precision grip.

---

1. http://theexplanation.com/human-life-7-1/

2. http://theexplanation.com/the-essence-of-being-human-is-revealed-by-museums-dedicated-to-life-activities/

To which I've added a versatile and non-exhaustive list of Museums which showcase a vast array of human accomplishments. Including one called the Imaginarium[3], dedicated to human imagination. There are numerous Imaginariums devoted to cultivating and stimulating the imagination to forward the goals of commerce, science, recreation, as well as spiritual and artistic endeavors.

The common denominator of these references to life of animals and humans is skeletal parts and the **brain** which runs and coordinates the body functions. That includes the main ones of **breathing** and **blood flow** to oxygenate and feed the body. Frankly, we can apply this description to both animal and human life. Yes, **when it comes to what I'll call** *physical life***, we're all the same**.

But when it comes to a human being, the above definition lacks an essential component without which we can't add the adjective: *human*. That is the all-important *mind*. Animals exhibit certain functions that we might equate with *mind*, and some scientists would say that this is the beginning of their development of consciousness.

Some could debate this for the rest of their lives. I have one question for them: **When will any animal, or group of animals, build a museum?** Or just a room in a museum? Or only one exhibit in a museum? Animals are not even close and never will be. We have a term to refer to this **extra-physical activity of animals: Instinct**. As defined by the dictionary: An innate, typically fixed pattern of behavior in animals in response to certain stimuli. Notice the *typically fixed pattern*. That's not to say animals can't take the initiative and make decisions; they can. I discussed this in *Inventory of the Universe* in the chapter about fauna[4]. But the point is there are **light-years between animal instinct and the human mind**.

---

3. https://en.wikipedia.org/wiki/Imaginarium

4. http://theexplanation.com/animal-intelligence-tool-makers-home-builders/

My diagnosis of this matter is that the underlying and all-encompassing uniqueness of humankind is their *mind*. Every human being that has walked the face of this Earth has been equipped with a mind. Section 9 of Inventory of the Universe was devoted in part to the mind of human's, as will be section 9 of this book, *Audit of the Universe*. We'll delve deeper into this subject without which it is impossible to understand how to establish peace and prosperity on Earth.

Think about this. We talk about the *time-space continuum*. That includes everything (animate and inanimate) in the *space* around us. On all sides, including in front and behind (length), on the left and right (width) and above and below us (height). *Time* represents the seconds, minutes, hours, days, months, years we have in the past, present, and future.

ONLY HUMANKIND can use and impact space and time. Animals cannot retain the notion of time and space. Yes, they live in the present, yes they migrate over vast distances (space), in season (time), according to an instinctive ritual. But they do not even begin to impact time and space other than with their immediate footprint and eating habits. **In the animal world, nothing changes,** animal life goes on, day in day out. That is the *typically fixed pattern* of instinct.

But, from **one day to the next (time)** men, women, children **transform**, each of our worlds (space) is reshaped, hopefully for the better, because humankind moves on. **Each human being constructs and shapes themselves; we're a little different each day.**

We progress because of one element: the mind with which each one of us is equipped. Returning to the Imaginarium museum, only human beings can form images and ideas in their heads and minds without input from their eyes and ears. Our human *senses* of smell, touch, etc. can

---

5. http://theexplanation.com/unique-brains-and-minds-for-each-human-but-brain-and-mind-unity-in-human-diversity/

conjure up images, concepts, solutions out of the blue, as we say. Consider young children with no toys; they can pick up anything and *make-believe*. That's the power of humans, that's the essence of being human.

I submit to you that **the central characteristic and basis for the definition of what HUMAN LIFE and what a HUMAN BEING IS is the POSSESSION of the MIND**. In chapter 9 of *Audit of the Universe*, we will discuss the state of an individual's mind. I'll just mention here, what you know, that a mind can be distorted or sick in which case we'd say a person isn't in their *right mind*. My point being, they still have a *mind*, it's just not functioning correctly—I will explain this situation.

In this chapter, I have briefly given you **my vision (that's what the mind can accomplish) of human life and what identifies a human being—the mind.** You might be thinking, *that's all conjecture*. Well, we're just getting into the crux of this matter, there's much more involved as you'll see.

For now, we conclude this chapter about human life. To do so, we need to come back to the focus of *Audit of the Universe*: To **evaluate the state of human life on Earth**, here and now. How are we treating human life? Is it edging closer to or further from peace and prosperity?

Below you will see links to some **articles about the general attitude toward the value of human life**. Is it held in esteem being adequately cared for? Considering we only have one life here and now, is humanity treating it with respect? Acknowledging its utmost importance, some would say its sacred nature?

Special Report: A business where human bodies were butchered, packaged, and sold https://buff.ly/2DotwHO I'm in the process of writing about human #life and especially our respect for it. This article deals with dead #human bodies, but it does reveal a callousness when it comes to life, #death, and financial gain. Somehow we've lost the admiration and reverence for #humanlife. Is it because of the individualistic society we live in? #theExplanation #AuditLife

We can't ban killer robots – it's already too late https://buff.ly/2gax-OfB #Chemical #warfare, atomic warfare, anti-personnel mines, all developed technology that (most) nations have outlawed because of their deadliness. Now come #killerrobots commanded only by their own #algorithm. They choose their #targets and can #kill indiscriminately. Why can #human minds develop such atrocities? #theExplanation #AuditMind #AuditViolence

Fight the silencing of gun research http://buff.ly/2ro19nF Beyond the evidence that the widespread presence of #guns causes more #deaths, the question is, why is there such a human fascination for weapons? #theExplanation #AuditViolence

Children bear the *disproportionate lethal impact* of the Syrian war, say researchers https://buff.ly/2zVf7l5 It's not just the number of #children killed. That's horrifying in itself. But, it's the impact of #war, fear, fleeing, #hunger on infant minds, and developing lives. A generation of scarred human beings. How can you build stable #families, #cities, #nations on rubble? Can we bomb and cajole people into peace?! #theExplanation #AuditViolence

Thankfully there are also positives regarding attitude towards human life:

Models of Respect https://buff.ly/2icnzse Short and wise article. "I want to see how people are treating other #people, human being to #humanbeing," says the author. It's all about #relationships. And it's part of behavior. Did you know that #behavior is the result of #humannature and #freewill? Think about it; relationships characterize #humans; it's part of our nature. Respect may or may not be exercised by each of us planetwide—it is a free will #choice as to whether we do it or don't do it. #theExplanation #AuditBehavior

Why Ikea's flatpack refugee shelter won design of the year https://buff.ly/2hzVTg2, making a difference for #refugees. Some positive news of #shelters and #dwellings that work. #Philanthropy is alive and helping where it can. #theExplanation #AuditBehavior

Now it's up to you. **What's your audit of planet-wide human life.** Are we shaping up or down? Next, we take a look at the human body and how we are treating ourselves and our physical health.

8. Audit Body

A Healthy Body for all Humans

Each human being wishes for a healthy body. We spend billions on technology and personal care. Are we making our dream come true?

Images of healthy bodies, both female and male, adorn our daily media. They're very often picture-perfect on the outside, but how are we treating our human bodies?

"You saw during our inventory of fauna[1] that **the animal kingdom is one of specialists**," Galacti remarks. "Cheetahs run faster than men. Monkeys climb higher. Tortoises live longer. Yet human bodies are still awe-inspiring."

---

1. http://theexplanation.com/animal-abilities-animal-communication/

We walk to Venice with the help of our traveling tour guide to the Gallerie dell'Accademia, where we view the muscled, graceful **image of DaVinci's** *Vitruvian Man*, the epitome of a healthy body. "Consider your eyes: not as sharp as a cat's, nor far-seeing as an eagle's, but **only your eyes can decipher writing.** Your hands are not as strong as a gorilla's, but unique on Earth in their capacity for fine manipulation. An elephant's legs are stronger, but only yours can dance. **Your bodies are wonderful machines, worthy of care and respect.**"

I begin to shrug off the compliment, as we humans so often do, but I am struck by the complexity of structure and engineering behind even just a simple movement. Galacti is right.

"Of all things in the universe," he continues, "**human bodies are truly the extension of the human mind.** You are their master, in control of how you treat it and how healthy you keep it, and to what ends you apply its impressive potential. I must ask now **how you steward your body.** How well do you care for it, both as a responsible individual in charge of a healthy body? And as an entire race caring for all humans in existence?"

Our Body of Knowledge

We tend to spend our money on what we most value, so the **$264 billion spent annually on health research worldwide seems to say that we humans do respect and appreciate our bodies.** This money goes toward new ways to extend life and health and to cure serious illnesses, as well as researching new technologies that help us accomplish the same goals.

As we audit the pros and cons of how each of us treats our healthy body, let's see where we are in 2018. Are the methods we're using to treat ourselves to remain vigorous and healthy regressing, stable or improving? **How is our general health doing?**

Antibiotics

Alexander Fleming discovered Penicillin in 1928, and we put the first medical antibiotic based on that discovery to work in the middle of World War 2. Antibiotics kill bacterial infections, which could become health-and-life threatening like pneumonia, pink eye, and blood poisoning. Before the widespread use of antibiotics, the three leading causes of human death were pneumonia, tuberculosis, and diarrhea dehydration from illnesses like dysentery or cholera. **The appropriate use of antibiotics cures all of these illnesses.** All have disappeared from the top causes of death in developed and practically all nations.

Antibiotic use does have a problematic side. Doctors often over-prescribe them, and patients tend to misuse them; this has led to a trend toward antibiotic resistance among bacteria. Strains of tuberculosis and staphylococci that are immune to many antibiotics are appearing in even the most advanced hospitals and countries. **Doctors fear a new age of epidemics stemming from the development of *superbugs* that our pharmaceutical weapons can't harm.**

Vaccines

Salk's polio vaccine ushered in another life-saving trend when he was able to prevent polio throughout the developed world. From that beginning, **we have developed vaccines to prevent more than 20 previously common illnesses.** Rates of childhood and adult infection for these illnesses have dropped dramatically since vaccination became a widespread practice. Some diseases—notably smallpox, diphtheria, and polio—are all but extinct. That means a more healthy body for many more people.

Vaccinations, like antibiotics, are not without their disadvantages. **Many doses inflict side effects,** including fever, soreness, and mild symptoms similar to the disease they are intended to prevent. About one child in a million is severely allergic to vaccines. Since vaccinations happen early in life, a severe reaction is often the first sign doctors, and families have of such an allergy.

Technologies for Treatment

Our history of medical technology dates back surprisingly far in time. Archaeologists have found evidence of skin grafts, false teeth, and even brain surgery from as early as the 3rd century BC.

Many of our modern medical wonders are simply improvements on existing devices and techniques. We build more accurate x-rays and sharper scalpels every year, but a few specimens of medical technology have opened broader potential. They won't create a healthy body, but they will go a long way to helping health.

- **Printable Organs** are a combination of stem cell technology with the 3-D printing that has already brought us printable tools and printable pizza. **By using stem cells from a patient as a model, scientists first printed a human kidney in 2011.** Since then, human testing is still in progress for both more complex organs and the process by which we can implant them into human patients. Though still limited because even the best 3-D printers can't yet produce objects as small as human capillaries—a vital element in the most critical organs—researchers hope to be able to create printed, on-demand, 100% compatible organs by 2020.
- **The Skin Gun** works similarly to printable organs, spraying **skin cells grown from stem cells onto a burned area,** and reducing recovery time from weeks to only a few days. Like printable organs, this technology is still in the prototyping stage. Still, it represents a hopeful development for the treatment of one of the most painful, infection-prone, and

lengthy injuries the human body can endure.

- **Vasalgel** is **a modern male contraceptive** that fills a small part of the vasa differentia with a gel that causes the sperm cell membrane to rupture. This advance began as a water treatment technique but is now undergoing human testing in India and primate testing in western countries. A reliable male contraceptive that lasts ten years and is quickly reversible could have wide-reaching effects on human health in overpopulated areas.

- **Bionics.** What was science fiction as recently as the 1990s is now rapidly becoming medical fact. Over the past few years, multiple successful tests have **allowed humans to control advanced prosthetic limbs using only mental commands**, just as they would a natural leg. More amazingly, those limbs do not have to be attached to the test subject's body. Instead, a wireless signal from a transmitter hooked into the patient's nervous system can control the limbs.

- **Medical Robotics** allows for **medical treatment with less error and more precision than humans.** As of 2014, we've prototyped robots to draw blood, manage telepresence for international experts or shut-in patients, and assist in a variety of nursing functions. Perhaps the most impactful robots will be the mobile communication robots like the Vasteras Giraff and the IRobot InTouch Health. These telepresence robots allow shut-in patients and practitioners in remote areas to communicate with healthcare professionals, from nurses to doctors to counselors, in real-time. This progress means both your grandmother at home alone, and a child in a developing nation could receive the same level of health care as they might receive in a major medical center.

Concerning technology and scientific progress, there have been tremendous strides over the past few decades to better care for and have a healthy body. There are drawbacks, and the question is, will we overcome them?

Body Care for our Physical Body.

Body care is a multi-billion dollar sector of the economy. In particular, it is a very personal issue. We all have an interest in caring for its well-being. How are we doing?

"We are creating real benefits via body care, as we've just observed, for the bodies of individuals and humanity in general," Galacti says. "But are there any secondary effects? Let's examine. Our audit of medical accomplishments tells one side of how humans value their bodies, but it's a rarified look. We see a bird's-eye view of what the experts and professionals do."

Daily Body Care and unforeseen Health Costs

I respond. "Like in our overall investigation, it's important that we see the whole picture and not just a piece of the puzzle. Now let's talk about the **day-to-day habits we have toward our bodies**. All intelligent beings are the sum of their habits. What do our habits say about us? Are they beneficial or detrimental to our health, welfare, and lifespans?"

Food for Thought

Consider a medieval farmer in Europe or Asia. He woke up near dawn to tend his fields and livestock, working until sunset made it too dark to see. Besides farming and shepherding, each day required him to chop wood, carry water and walk for miles. Each calorie he took in by eating required hard physical labor to produce and earn. **Those calories were fresh and mostly unprocessed** and included many fruits, vegetables, and whole grains. Excellent for body care.

Compare this to a modern executive's relationship with food. He wakes before dawn and returns home after dark, but his workday consists of sitting in his car or sitting at a desk. His calories—of which he often consumes more than he expends—are **commonly prepackaged and preprocessed**. His diet contains fewer whole grains, fruits or vegetables, and more fat, sugar, and salt.

Our relationship with food has changed significantly over the centuries. What used to require a thousand calories to produce now takes fifty calories to buy. Whole grain loaves from grain we grew have given way to soft, sugary bread we buy from a rack at the store, or a "Happy Meal" bought and consumed in the car. This imbalance, like the other imbalances we've examined in or audit, causes problems—in this case, illnesses like obesity, diabetes, and heart disease. **In developed nations worldwide, the cost of medical issues related to overeating far exceeds the costs of malnutrition.**

In some cases, the best food choices for our bodies are easy to see but more difficult to enact. A mother in an impoverished neighborhood of a major city like London, Beijing, or Chicago **might know to avoid processed foods and to prepare fresh vegetables for her children**—but well-supplied grocery stores and farmer's markets are few and far between in a slum. The economic realities of access to nutritious foods force her to feed her children with wilting lettuce, frozen peas, and bags of processed carbohydrates. Not to mention foods that lack the necessities of essential nutrients like proteins, trace elements, vitamins, and essential minerals that body care demands.

Drinking soda instead of water is unhealthy, but the realities complicate that decision. In much of Mexico, tap water is unsafe to drink. Much like our medieval ancestors drank beer because it was safer than untreated water, many Mexicans drink soda because it is cheaper and easier to obtain than safe drinking water. Increased consumption of soft drinks in Mexico has happened concurrently with the country becoming the world's worst in obesity per capita.

A similar health problem appeared in Central America and Africa when food companies first introduced baby formula to developing nations in those regions. Although the **formula is a healthy alternative to breast milk, this is only the case when made using safe drinking water.** The unintended consequences of bringing powdered formula to a community without safe water included as many as one million infant deaths from malnutrition and diarrhea.

Staying fit, use It or lose It

Keeping our bodies healthy requires two sides of a behavioral coin. **On the opposite side from eating right is getting sufficient exercise.** French health resources recommend walking a minimum of 10,000 steps each day, while American information pegs the minimum at 20 minutes of moderate exercise daily. Fitness professionals recommend

30 minutes of cardiovascular workouts three days a week, plus vigorous resistance training on three other days. The details aren't as important as their clear consensus: **daily strenuous activity is an integral part of treating our body care with respect.**

When allowed to remain sedentary, body care is not at its best. Insufficient activity leads to an increased risk of obesity, heart disease, diabetes, and some forms of cancer—as well as various mental illnesses, including anxiety and depression disorders. Remaining active after turning 50 can slow—and in some cases reverse—age-related degeneration of muscle and bone.

Our children are a telling illustration of how this growing inactivity affects peace and prosperity by limiting our health and wellness. Since 1999, the number of obese teens in developed countries has increased to where nearly one in five boys is obese. That boy lives daily with the exertion of carrying extra fat, the discomfort of needing two seats on the school bus, and being ridiculed by classmates and often by teachers. As an adult, he will suffer even more physical discomfort, be discriminated against for jobs and promotions, and likely die early from heart disease, diabetes, or several kinds of cancer.

In 2010 alone, we **spent $665 billion worldwide on exercise, nutrition, fitness, and weight loss programs.** Athletic events like the Olympics and World Cup attract audiences of billions each year, and admiration is worldwide for elite athletes in all nations. We idolize these athletic paragons, precisely because we value and respect the importance of health and wellness.

We show that appreciation and respect in the widespread popularity of programs that encourage physical fitness. The "Exercise is Medicine[1]" initiative is an example of one such program. Practiced in 31 countries, promoted by national governments and supported with private dona-

---

1. http://exerciseismedicine.org/

tions, it combines a free-for-everybody "Action Guide" with **incentives for individuals to take responsibility for their own health**. Programs like this exist throughout the developed world, led by medical professionals, government officials, and corporate leaders alike. They are exemplary in the real promotion of body care.

Through these programs and many other influences[2], men and women have found the motivation and resources to make positive changes to their health. It doesn't matter whether it's running, fitness, gym, dancing, indoor, outdoor, personal or team fitness programs, it's your body and each one's decision for personal body care. Initiatives like this demonstrate that we are willing to take action toward better health if given even a small push. The organizations we participate in are also becoming aware of the necessary vitality for the physical body. We'll see whether this dynamism grows or fades away.

---

2. http://womensrunning.competitor.com/category/girlfriends-guide-to-running

Addiction Affects our Bodies

Addiction and regular use of pharmaceuticals, light, and hard drugs among all ages and sexes, especially adolescents, have become a real dilemma.

Addiction to harmful substances hurts the body that uses the drug, the family that loves the addict, and the person's ability to make positive changes in the future.

Addiction and abuse drugs are sadly common across all cultures and countries. Different substances have different effects and side effects and have been more or less popular than others.

The Cycle of Abuse and Addiction

Nicotine

Nicotine, delivered primarily via tobacco use or products meant to help curb tobacco addiction, is a stimulant connected with insomnia, digestive problems, and symptoms similar to the flu. Smoking, by far the most common form of taking nicotine, has been definitively shown to be a chief cause of lung cancer.

According to 2012 estimates, **over 1.1 billion use nicotine regularly**. If we collected them all in one place, their numbers would exceed the population of India and rival that of China.

Caffeine

The most commonly used and abused drug in the world, caffeine is taken most often in beverage form with the coffee or tea people worldwide drink to begin their mornings or in many types of carbonated soft drinks. Adverse effects of caffeine use include increased blood pressure, sleep problems, and mood swings. Can we call this an addiction?

Around the world, we consume approximately 120,000 tons of caffeine annually. Though people get their caffeine in a variety of forms, we can understand that amount best by knowing it's enough to make one trillion 8-oz cups of coffee. Every year, humans consume enough caffeine to make two and a half cups of Joe for every star in the Milky Way galaxy.

Alcohol

According to the WHO, approximately 140 million people worldwide ruin their lives, lose their families, and face legal problems, including arrest and lawsuits. They are at serious risk of a host of illnesses that harm the body and reduce the quality of their lives even after they recover from uncontrolled addiction.

Illegal Drugs

Marijuana, opiates and opioids, cocaine and hallucinogens like LSD, Ecstasy, and Psylocibin, can have **devastating effects on the mind**, body, and social context of a user. Not to mention the legal risks associated with using an illegal substance. Despite this risk, approximately 300 million people—twice the population of Japan—regularly use these drugs.

In our audit of the body, it's worth looking at how we use harmful and addictive substances, how often, and under what circumstances. *Pills* take many forms like using *wonder drugs* to cure illnesses, vitamin supplements to improve our health, and addictive poisons for recreation and escape.

On this *Audit of the Universe Hashtags page that corroborates The Explanation[1],* there are some up-to-date articles about addiction (#Audit-Drugs). Below is a list of recent headlines with short links to peruse these eye-opening articles.

- Microdosers say tiny hits of LSD make your work and life better http://buff.ly/2t0jcUu [2]
- Fish on Drugs May Help Cure Opioid Addiction https://buff.ly/2eRrpTa
- Can Repairing Your Brain's Wiring Help You Fight Addiction? https://buff.ly/2eR4HdV
- Opioid Addiction: Is This a War We Can Win? https://buff.ly/2wsd1eP
- Performance Enhancing Drugs in Everyday Life https://buff.ly/2hxV9WA [3]
- Olympics: Evidence found in Sochi drugs probe to charge athletes https://buff.ly/2iu0fGU

---

1. *http://theexplanation.com/audit-of-the-universe-hashtags-that-corroborate-the-explanation/*

2. http://buff.ly/2t0jcUu

3. https://buff.ly/2hxV9WA

- Opiate deaths demand serious action https://buff.ly/2Az4LIB

Longer Lives, Healthier Communities

"Just as the glasses of your environment and life on earth are filling or emptying, **decisions about our bodies empty or fill the glass of health**," Galacti says. "What might be a fair judge of whether it is filling or emptying?"

"Our lifespans," I say. "It's not a perfect measure, but it's a metric we can examine."

Early humans had a life expectancy of 26-30 years by science's best estimates, and that expectancy has grown steadily beginning in the late 19th century. By 1900, people in the developed world could expect to see their 48th birthday, and **modern man lives well into their 80s.**

Those longer lives often come with the benefit of a longer time when a person is active and engaged in life. Fifty years ago, most men died within five years of retiring. **Today, seniors provide a wealth of benefits to a community, society, and the world as a whole.** In the developed world, the phenomenon of retiree volunteers now comprises an estimated 30 to 50 percent of hours provided for aid organizations at home and abroad.

"Talk about a net benefit for peace and prosperity," Galacti opines. "**Seniors stay active and continue to have new experiences**—which increases both life and health. Their work benefits less fortunate people all over the world."

"Everybody wins," I agree.

Nearly every community has a story of how **active seniors benefit the whole.**

- In Paris, France, the university population is so high that student housing is overfull. **Seniors are letting out spare rooms to students**; this benefits both since the senior has company and more variety in her life, and the student has the benefit of an experienced mentor.
- Programs throughout the United States allow **single mothers in school to visit retirement centers several times per week.** The senior residents get *lap time* with the babies while the moms get a needed break to finish homework or simply relax.
- **Seniors also help seniors in the US and Europe** by volunteering to drive their peers to appointments, run errands, or simply perform house visits.
- So many retirees are still active and interested in engaging with the world that **volunteer tourism for seniors is a multibillion-dollar industry**. It brings retirees from North America and Europe to help with service projects throughout Asia, Africa, and Latin America.

In eastern countries like Japan, China, and India, senior service travel is less of a trend. It isn't because seniors from these nations don't benefit their societies. On the contrary, **participating is already a big part of their culture.**

- In **India**, retired grandparents often come and live with new parents to help change diapers and stay up at night during that intensive and exhausting first year of life.
- **Chinese** elders garner high respect and play a role in decisions for the family ranging from financial matters to arranging marriages.
- In **Japan**, seniors volunteered to participate in the cleanup for the Fukushima nuclear disaster because they would not live long enough to suffer the long-term health problems that would come from that work.

"**Longer lives, when healthy and engaged, are indeed a benefit to the individual and her community**. But is so much life an entirely unmixed blessing?" Galacti wonders aloud.

The social support systems in most developed nations function **by taxing the working-aged population and using the money to provide for the retired**. If lifespans increase substantially, those systems as they exist will not be sustainable.

Governments in the United States and Europe are already proposing and passing laws to avert the disaster that will come if **the number of seniors who need social support exceeds the resources available to support them**. Without significant changes to those systems, seniors might live without sufficient food and medications.

Weighing the Balance

"The glass of your lifespan seems to be filling with each new medical advance," Galacti says. "That's probably a good thing on the whole. Now **how about the rest of man's relationship with their bodies?** Does humanity make decisions that fill the glass, or empty it? Will the trend toward longer healthier lives continue, or has it seen a high water mark? What does this answer say about our overall quest for peace and prosperity throughout the universe?"

We're going to take a **much more in-depth look at how humans view the human body**. I have to say it is an ongoing controversy that profoundly impacts the direction of our inquiry as to how to bring peace and prosperity to Earth. Along with that, we are going to discuss the **role of the human hand**—it's a unique member of our body.

9. Audit Brain - Mind

Is the Mind Part of a Body Organ?

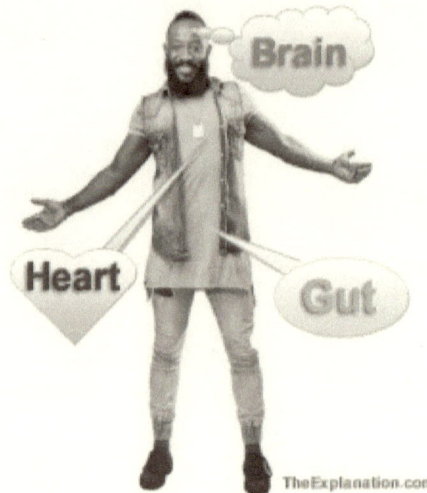

Are the Brain, Heart and Gut, which are parts of the Body, Mind?

Brain

Heart

Gut

TheExplanation.com

Body and mind—are they the same? May sound unimportant, but therein lies the question: Is there a non-physical component in human beings? Or are we just totally physical flesh and bone?

Body and mind, what is the relationship between them? **We use the word** *cognitive* **to refer to** *mental* **activities. Where does the** *mental* **take place?** Is it solely in the brain, heart, and gut? Each has incredibly inter-connected neurons—is this vast network together body and mind?

The Explanation has audited the way we do, or don't, take care of our bodies. The pros and cons of how we treat what genetics has bequeathed to us for a certain number of years. Whether it's our food and liquid intake or what we subject our bodies to, here's the question for our audit. **As a society progressing in the 21st century, are we subjecting our bodies to improved or detrimental treatment?** It is not just an individual evaluation but a global overview of this audit as we are doing with the rest of the analyses we're broaching throughout this book.

But these last three sections of *Audit of the Universe* (7-9) and the next book, *Audit of Humankind*, are more than just a *state of affairs* evaluation. Starting with the previous chapter, Human Life[1], I need to help us **define more precisely what each component in the Universe is.** Remember, our primary question: How can we bring peace and prosperity to Earth?

To answer this, **we** need to zero in on who and what on Earth can contribute to not only answering this question but especially **who can engender such a state of bliss.**

In section 7 on Human Life, we saw that philosophers, performing an analysis, reached the following resume about **what defines humankind[2]: Civilization, language, abstract thought, morals, ethics, perfectability, technology, the ability to analyze.**

When considered together, this list of human characteristics represents different **facets of the same gem: cognitive capacity beyond the physical mechanics of the brain.** All animals have bodies and brains and are capable of phenomenal prowesses, but only humans have a mind. Only humankind—with body and mind—has civilization, language, abstract thought, morals, ethics, perfectability, technology, and the ability to analyze.

---

1. http://theexplanation.com/human-life-7-1/

2. **http://theexplanation.com/human-life-7-1/**

I shall return to all these human characteristics during the following sections, starting with this discussion of the human body. We'll see some aspects of each of our bodies. Why? Because **all humans,** no matter where we are or what our origins and beliefs are, **without exception, have a human body, including a brain, a heart, a gut, and hands.** You'll see why I refer to a *gut.*

Sam's Confession

Now for a confession. I'm not an expert by any means in any of the areas I elaborated **in *Inventory* or *Audit*.** These are what I'd call *scientific* explanations. **I've synthesized subjects that I've studied, read, and received assistance.** I've given you the references to verify the affirmations. Frankly, my intention is not to provide you with every last detail about space, atmosphere, water, land, flora, humans, etc. So many other experts do excellent in-depth studies, let them give you the nuts-and-bolts, the macro, and micro of these essential domains.

The goal of *The Explanation* is to show you how ALL these subjects intermingle to form coherent completeness. To reveal how each aspect of the Universe is an essential, required, even obligatory, piece in a perfectly fitted puzzle.

Body and Mind

For now, though, I feel I need to make you aware of a profound controversy that involves the body and the mind. Here's a quote[3]. "**Cognitive** neuroscience is the scientific field that is concerned with the study of

---

3. https://en.wikipedia.org/wiki/Cognitive_neuroscience

the *biological processes* and aspects that underlie cognition, with a specific focus on the *neural connections* in the brain which are involved in **mental processes."**

I don't expect you to understand what this is all about. However, I have emphasized the quote because I want you to see the relationship between the *body* (*italics*) and the **mind** (**bold**). This statement says that the *body* is involved in **mental** (mind) processes.

You need to know that today some believe and clearly state, with their proof that **ALL mental activity is initiated by and remains solely within the BODY.** The brain, neural system, as well as the 'heart' and 'gut' (feelings) participate in these mental processes. **The body is the beginning and end of all human mental composition.**

Here's such a quote[4]—including the conclusions to which such thinking leads:

'But with the rise of affective neuroscience and **embodied cognition** we are now able to offer much more robust and compelling versions of the third story, At my most radical, I would now claim that, not only are *the gods and spirits* **non-existent** (even though they may still have their uses), but **the unconscious is dead too.** We may choose to continue using it as a metaphorical or poetic way of talking, but thar ain't no such animal. There are myriad processes in the body that never lead to conscious experience, but there is no real, identifiable place or agent inside us that is a separate source of impetus from consciousness and

---

4. https://www.amazon.com/Intelligence-Flesh-Your-Needs-Thinks/dp/0300223471/
ref=pd_sim_14_4?_encod-
ing=UTF8&pd_rd_i=0300223471&pd_rd_r=NSWWFTJ5HB4AFRMRQX-
GA&pd_rd_w=45nwD&pd_rd_wg=yftL2&psc=1&refRID=NSWWFTJ5HB4AFRMRQX-
GA

reason. **Like *the mind, the unconscious* is a place-saver, a dummy explanation**. It is like a temporary filling in a tooth, put there till something better comes along. **And now it has**. (the emphasis is by Sam)

My understanding of what Guy Claxton is saying in his book, Intelligence in the Flesh[5], is this. **The body includes everything to do with the mind. Everything else is non-existent**. Elements like *mind, unconscious, gods,* and *spirits* can be thrown out and considered hogwash. I will add God because if there are no gods, there is also no God. Claxton might also be referring to ghosts, extra-sensory phenomena, etc. and I must add the *spirit in man* and the *Holy Spirit*. Many of you are aware of these spirits, which the Explanation will expound in *Origin of the Universe* and *Humankind*.

With one paragraph at the outset of his book, **Claxton has wiped the slate clean of all *outside of the body* phenomena** having the slightest impact on cognition—mental activity. Not only do they not have any effect, but they are *dummy explanations*. To put it in my own words, **he eliminates anything and everything *spiritual***.

Let me give you two more quotes, this first one from the Oxford dictionary[6]:

Cognition is "the mental action or process of acquiring knowledge and understanding through **thought**, experience, and the senses."

And the second **focuses on *thought***, which is an essential part of the mental process. What is *thinking*? [7]

---

5. https://www.amazon.com/Intelligence-Flesh-Your-Needs-Thinks/dp/0300223471/

ref=pd_sim_14_4?_encod-

ing=UTF8&pd_rd_i=0300223471&pd_rd_r=NSWWFTJ5HB4AFRMRQX-

GA&pd_rd_w=45nwD&pd_rd_wg=yftL2&psc=1&refRID=NSWWFTJ5HB4AFRMRQX-

GA

6. https://en.oxforddictionaries.com/definition/cognition

"Thought refers to ideas or arrangements of ideas that are the result of the process of thinking. Though thinking is an activity considered essential to humanity, **there is no consensus as to how it is defined or understood.**"

Because thought underlies many human actions and interactions, understanding its physical and metaphysical origins, processes, and effects have been a longstanding goal of many academic disciplines including linguistics, psychology, neuroscience, **philosophy**, artificial intelligence, biology, sociology, and **cognitive science.**

Cognition involves *thinking,* a study by various branches of cognitive science of which *embodied cognition*, embraced by Claxton, is one (see his quote above). All the above branches of science and I see they've added philosophy to the list have come to **NO consensus**. Not only is there no conclusion, but there is downright **opposition, contradiction, and confusion among scientists and philosophers about what and where cognition is.**

You need to **be very careful with affirmative statements about the extent of the body, brain, heart, and gut when it comes to mental and mind activities.** There's an involvement with the body. But the study of the cognitive, which some say is the last, yet foremost frontier of discovery goes far beyond scanners and electron microscopes—observation and measuring.

I want to leave this section about body and mind with a point for you to think about: **Where, in humans, is imagination located?** Can that be observed and quantified? That is the role of science. **What about** *Eureka moments, ideas,* **and** *solutions*—**can we show what part of the body originates and stores them?**

---

7. https://en.wikipedia.org/wiki/Thought

We will get into a part of this piece of the puzzle in the next chapter and *Audit of Humankind*. However, the full explanation is in *Origin of the Humankind*. There, **I explain why each of us human beings has the body and mind we do and what their origin is**. You'll learn why there is such a need for scientists to explain that ALL ASPECTS of a human being—mind and body—are wrapped up SOLELY IN THE PHYSICAL BODY. I guarantee you; this is quite a story in itself.

HANDS

Let's conclude this chapter by focusing on our hands. They serve our every need. They are the instruments of our actions—human tools. **Hands allow us to manipulate the world so that we can fulfill our wishes**. Hands, as part of human bodies, set us apart from animals.

Only humans can:

- Gently wipe away tears, your own and those of a loved one.
- Grab a hammer and pound a nail in straight.
- Pack your clothes in a suitcase and then stack them in the trunk of a car.
- Wrap a fragile gift and tie a decorative bow.
- Peel a fruit, pluck a chicken, cut it up and transform it into a mouth-watering recipe.
- Perform a million other coordinated, dexterous, manipulative movements.

This *body part* doesn't get much thought; it's often overlooked. If you want a deeper understanding of the effect of *hands* on humans, especially nowadays, with the switch of their use away from *manual* activities to *key-punching* activities, then I suggest you peruse Hands by Darian Leader[8]. In *Origin of Humankind,* I'll discuss **the relationship between human hands and the human mind. Body and mind.** I'd even say they go hand-in-hand.

Here's a treat for you, **a video of Darci Lynn's quarter-final performance[9] on America's Got Talent.** For the sake of this chapter, please focus on her left hand and see how she *manipulates* Oscar. **She transmits emotion to this chunk of tissue.** She makes Oscar come alive by moving his hands adroitly in conjunction with his whole body, the music, and the performance. You can also watch her right hand and see how she choreographs Oscar's head and body for a real-life singing act. In Darci's first audition, Mel B said of the puppet Petunia, "I guess she's just like you." Well, yes, because Darci can transmit that inner part of herself to a rag doll and make it act humanlike with her hands.

I suggest you also watch the semi-finals and finals (which she won) and stay focused on her hands. I don't know if she's ambidextrous or not, but the emotions she transmits to Petunia and Oscar through the movement of her hands is nothing short of amazing. Hands and emotions - body and mind - in perfect sync. Hands set humankind apart from any and every other form of life.

---

8. https://www.theguardian.com/books/2016/may/21/darian-leader-how-technology-changing-our-hands

9. https://youtu.be/MdWHTes65Zg

Mind, a Body Part, or Somewhere Else?

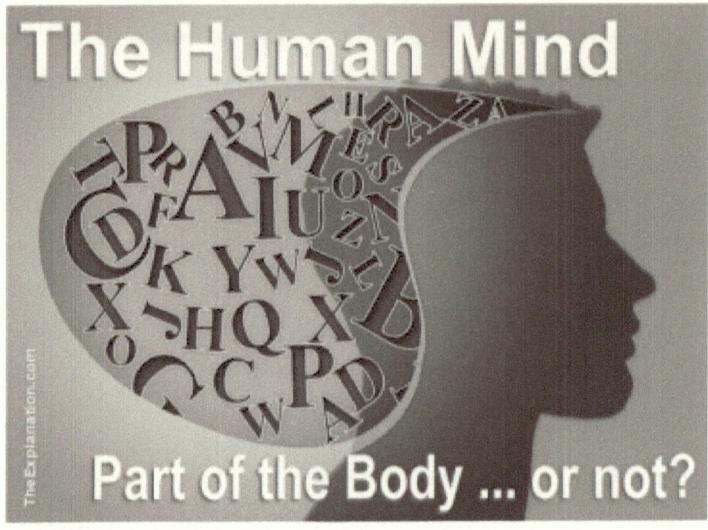

The human mind, the last and biggest enigma yet to be solved. What is it? How does it function? Today we will see its location.

The human mind is an essential, if not the critical piece, in the puzzle of the Universe. *The Explanation* proposes to put all the puzzle pieces of the Universe together in a coherent, complete way. That's quite an undertaking. To do so, *The Explanation* started to define what the fundamental puzzle pieces are *in the book Inventory of the Universe[1]*. *Audit of the Universe* explains more about how these pieces interlock and primarily how humanity is affecting them.

---

1. *http://theexplanation.com/inventory/read-all-the-content-of-inventory-of-the-universe-online/*

Let's discuss the human mind. That is a tautology, two terms that mean the same thing. Having a mind defines what a human being is; humans alone possess a mind. A mind makes a human, human.

Think about this statement. **Everything humans do is because they alone possess a mind**. Everything humans do can only be explained based on the mind.

Scrutinize these 160+ following puzzle pieces. How can we explain ALL these words wholly and coherently? Answer these questions regarding each piece: **Where can you find these intangible elements in the human body?** Are they part of the human body? Are they part of a member of the human body? **What's the common denominator**, the curvature of each piece, that makes them all fit together in humans, perfectly?

Acceptance, Acedia, Acute stress reaction, Adoration, Aesthetic emotions, Affection, Affective science, Ambivalence, Amusement, Anger, Angst, Anguish, Annoyance, Anticipation, Antipathy, Anxiety, Apathy, Arousal, Artistic inspiration, Aversion to happiness, Awe, Biological basis of love, Boredom, Calmness, Cognitive bias in animals, Compassion, Confidence, Confusion, Contempt, Contentment, Courage, Curiosity, Defeatism, Depression (mood), Desire, Diligence, Disappointment, Disgust, Distrust, Doubt, Ecstasy (emotion), Embarrassment, Emotion, Emotion and memory, Emotion classification, Emotion in animals, Emotion perception, Emotion work, Emotional bias, Emotional competence, Emotional contagion, Emotional exhaustion, Emotional expression, Emotional intelligence, Emotional literacy, Emotional security, Emotional self-regulation, Emotions and culture, Emotions in virtual communication, Empathy, Emptiness, Enthusiasm, Envy, Epiphany (feeling), Euphoria, Euthymia (medicine), Evolution of emotion, Fear, Forgiveness, Four Cornerstone Model of Emotional Intelligence, Frustration, Functional accounts of emotion, Gratification, Gratitude, Grief, Group emotion, Guilt (emotion), Han (cultural), Happiness, Hatred, Homeostatic emotion, Homesickness, Hope, Horror and terror, Hostility, Hubris, Humiliation, Hysteria, Infatuation, Insult, Interest (emotion), Interpersonal attraction, Irritability, Isolation (psychology), Jealousy, Jealousy in art, Joy, Limerence, Loneliness, Love, Lust, Melancholia, Meta-emotion, Mimpathy, Miscarriage and grief, Mono no aware, Mourning sickness, Neuroticism, Nostalgia, Oculesics, Optimism, Outrage (emotion), Outrage porn, Pain, Panic, Panic disorder, Paranoia, Passion (emotion), Pessimism, Pity, Pleasure, Pride, Psychomotor agitation, Rage (emotion), Recluse, Regret, Regulation of emotion, Relaxation (psychology), Remorse, Resentment, Revenge, Reverence (emotion), Righteous indignation, Rush (psychology), Sadness, Saudade, Schadenfreude, Sehnsucht, Self-confidence, Self-love, Self-pity, Sentimentality, Shame, Shyness, Social emotions, Social sharing of emotions, Sociology of emotions, Solitude, Sorrow (emotion), Spite (sentiment), Stimulation, Suffering, Surprise (emotion), Suspense, Suspicion (emotion), Sympathy, Trust (emotion), Vicarious embarrassment, Weltschmerz, Wonder (emotion), Worry, Zest (positive psychology),

Yes, I'm trying to impress you. Impress on your *mind* the realization that this vast diversity of emotions, sentiments, moods, psychological, and medical attitudes has a specific and definite position in the billions-of-pieces puzzle that constitutes the Universe.

To understand humans and their role in the Universe, you must be able to make sense of these various attitudes. How about their opposition and intensity? Most of them are necessary and proper reactions at a given point in time, under particular circumstances. How do we explain that precisely these same attitudes animate all human beings worldwide, whether they've lived in tightly-knit communities or remote hinterlands? What is the common denominator that has brought about this ever-so fundamental observation?

I know you're not a doctor, psychologist or scientist—but you know where your arms, your brain, your heart, and your gut are. We talked about in the previous chapter[2]. So, here's something we hear all the time: Think! **Where do these moods, sentiments, and emotions reside in your body**, if they're in your body at all?

Yes, these are a lot of questions—and I will answer them. There is **so much contradiction and misguided information out there.** However, if you **come down to basics, you can home in on the answer**. I really would like you to come to the proper conclusion yourself. It's there to see, so here are some clues to guide you.

Look at this page filled with idioms about the human mind[3]. Can you substitute *brain* for *mind* in these idioms and have the same meaning? Below are a few examples from that page:

- State of mind
- Piece of one's mind
- Speak one's mind
- It's mind-boggling
- Be of one mind
- and on and on it goes
- I could politely say, *you're out of your mind* if you can't see that even colloquial language differentiates the brain and the mind. It places the *human mind* on a level that is higher than the physical organ we call the brain. The human mind is where the intellect, the thinking process, and reasoning take place.

---

2. http://theexplanation.com/body-and-mind-are-the-brain-heart-and-gut-all-body-organs-the-mind/

3. https://idioms.thefreedictionary.com/mind

Here's another list of about 100 action verbs performed by the cognitive[4]—the human mind. Of course, there's a relationship between the brain and other parts of the body which accomplish the physical execution. You write and repair with your hands, you explain with your mouth, but **your mind makes the decisions of what to write and how you repair or explain**.

You can group the above cognitive actions into six categories: **Knowledge, comprehension, application, analysis, synthesis, and evaluation—all activities of the human mind**. Very similar to these: Believing, blaming, catastrophism, determination, egotism, imagining, judging, jumping to conclusions, negativism, positivism, stress, or stubbornness. Neither your brain, nor the neuronal circuits, nor your heart, nor your gut—all organs in your body—imagine, judge, believe or originate negativism or egotism.

Robots and AI

The **latest technological craze is robots and artificial intelligence** (AI). Predictions are that within 5-10-20-50 years; we'll create a robot that will be able to supplant a human. In other words, humans are replaceable. There are even sci-fi movies with this theme[5], 2001: A Space Odyssey, with HAL 9000 being the precursor.

Here's an article that lauds the ability of computers that whop humans at intricate games[6] like chess and Go. After a month, a computer had developed its poker game (mastering the bluff and deceptiveness of this game) to the point of winning 1.7 million fictitious dollars from four professional poker players.

---

4. http://www.cme.hsc.usf.edu/latestdocs/06-BloomsTaxonomy.pdf

5. https://en.wikipedia.org/wiki/List_of_artificial_intelligence_films

6. https://newatlas.com/ai-2017-beating-humans-games/52741/

Oh yes, computers can learn and develop better programs and methods as our poker playing machine demonstrates. What you have to realize is that **it is all about computations.** Whereas **a human chess player can think about a few dozen moves, a computer can think about millions of options.** The more it perfects its computational capabilities, which it does by playing and teaching itself, the better it gets, and the more readily it wins.

But, here's the question, way beyond algorithms and computations. **Can a robot, which is nothing more than a dressed-up computer, ever develop the attitudes, moods, sentiments, emotions, and feelings we've briefly discussed in this blog post?** Those attitudes are just a part of what identifies human beings (the first section of *Audit of Humankind* is about the singularity of humankind). Each of our personalities, so different one from another, is a combination of all these sentiments and feelings. Can and will robots express human nature and character?

I believe you possess the mind frame to cut through the hype and answer that question. The human body is not a computer. **Brain health and that of other organs can inhibit or enhance moods**, emotions, and cognitive activity. **But the human mind is not a body part;** it is not *part of a part; it* is not a combination of components; it is not a network of parts. When we're talking about the mind, we include *common sense.* You have common sense, the ability to put two and two together, and trump scientific jargon with critical thinking.

As we develop the definition of the human mind, I'll give you quotes from open-minded scientists who have looked at the pros and cons and come to this conclusion.

I will show you **WHY the human mind is the focal point of every-thing in our physical Universe**. Its uppermost role in the drama that's playing out on Earth. In the next chapter, we'll see how humankind is treating this gem, this all-important piece of the puzzle.

Mental Health. State of the World

Mental health is probably the most precious possession each of us owns. You are your mind, and your mind is you.

Mental health is a significant issue nowadays. I dare say we tend to pay more attention to our bodies than our minds. Are we taking care of the physical and letting the mind go to pot? Concretely and metaphorically?

The last chapter referred to a list **of** diverse emotions, sentiments, moods, psychological, and medical attitudes. I asked you the question: **Where do these moods, feelings, and emotions reside in your body if they're in your body at all?**

This book and the next one *Audit of humankind* have a double objective:

1. To address the *state of the union of individuals, nations, and the universe*. How is humankind doing in a particular area? In this chapter: **How are our minds faring?**

2. To define more precisely the *pieces of the puzzle*. In this chapter: The mind. We're continuing to turn over parts of the whole to make it clear what's at stake. If we don't know the basics, how can we go on to the more complex? If we don't possess all the pieces of the puzzle, how can we possibly put it all together and see a final clear picture? With that in mind, **what is the mind?**

State of Mind

Mental disorders refer to a state of mind; they will point us in the direction of what is involved with the *mind*. Mental health and aspects associated with the mind are very complex and encompass numerous phenomena that are difficult to explain. I will point out some of them.

Let's go straight to the comprehensive picture with the World Health Organization[1]: Depression tops the list of causes of ill-health. *30 MARCH 2017 | GENEVA* - **Depression is the leading cause of ill-health and disability worldwide**. According to the latest estimates from WHO, more than 300 million people are now living with depression. That's an increase of more than 18% between 2005 and 2015.

WHO statistics paint a bleak picture[2]. Common mental health disorders refer to a range of anxiety and depressive conditions. Global estimates indicate that 4.4% of the worldwide population suffers from a

---

1. http://www.who.int/mediacentre/news/releases/2017/world-health-day/en/

2. http://apps.who.int/iris/bitstream/10665/254610/1/WHO-MSD-MER-2017.2-eng.pdf?ua=1

depressive disorder, and 3.6% from an anxiety disorder. We're talking about **almost 600,000,000 people.** By comparison, Europe's population is about 760 million people.

Similar situations are prevalent **in the USA[3] and UK[4]: At any time, one in six adults has a mental health** condition, and one in 100 has a severe mental illness. People with mental ill-health die younger, and a higher proportion has poor physical health compared to the general population. These differences are most profound for people with serious mental illnesses, such as psychosis or bipolar disorder. They die about 10 to 17 years earlier than the average populace.

This chapter is probably the most depressing I've ever written and might ever write. There are gigantic catastrophes like the earthquake and subsequent tsunami that snuffed out 230,000 lives in Asia and East Africa in 2004. But, there is no other long-term health illness as debilitating and perplexing as mental disorders.

Here's a website reference to mental disorders[5] that delves into **some major but common types like** anxiety disorders mood disorders, psychotic disorders, eating disorders, impulse control, and addiction disorders, personality disorders, obsessive-compulsive disorder, post-traumatic stress disorder and some less common types of mental illnesses including Stress response syndromes emotional or behavioral symptoms because of stressful situations. Dissociative disorders due to overwhelming stress, factitious disorders, complaining of physical symptoms to place oneself in the role of a person needing help. Sexual and gender disorders affecting sexual desire and performance. Somatic symptom disorders, experiencing physical symptoms with no known

---

3. https://www.nimh.nih.gov/health/statistics/mental-illness.shtml

4. https://www.nuffieldtrust.org.uk

5. https://www.webmd.com

medical cause. Tic disorders display repeated uncontrolled body movements: sleep-related problems, variations of dementia, including Alzheimer's disease.

It, unfortunately, points out that mental health disorders are growing faster among kids than adults[6]. This chapter has the intention of making you aware of mind-related matters that can affect mental health both positively and negatively. It focuses on the psychological, which is associated with the mind.

It does stay general because **my goal is to motivate you to think about practical everyday situations**, emotions, thoughts, and activities in your environs. I would like you to realize we take a lot of this for granted, but it's much deeper than you might think. There are a lot of unanswered questions, and **I don't get into answers about the *mind* in *Audit of the Universe*. I'll go very far in showing you and affirming that it is not a part of the physical brain**—not any part of the body.

You can read ***Origin of Humankind,* where show you what the mind is and why each human must have a mind and what its purpose is.** In the meantime, ponder the origin of the following *phenomena* related to the mental.

One has to be very careful when talking about these subjects because **they are related to medical and religious fields.** Many go so far as to **feel that through these mind-practices, they can reach peace and even God.** They use practices like demon attribution, uncontrolled rhythmic dancing, rhythmic drums and other instruments, exorcism, personal near-death experiences, out-of-body and paranormal experiences[7], speaking in tongues, automatic writing, composing, singing, painting, and other incoherent practices like visions and interpreting

---

6. https://www.webmd.com/mental-health/news/20131127/mental-health-disorders-growing-faster-among-kids-than-adults-study

7. https://en.wikipedia.org/wiki/Out-of-body_experience#Induced

dreams. Other psychological mind phenomena include multi-person-alities, hypnotism, mesmerism, black magic, reading minds, fortune-telling, charlatanism, trances, transcendental meditation, and mindful-ness.

All of the above practices help people reach a *high*. There's no doubt that from a human perspective, lives are being changed by these experiences, like Ayahuasca and its healing retreats[8]. People do reach more peace, serenity, calmness, They can and do replace anxiety and guilt. Yes, there are pros, but are there cons, even unsuspected consequences? Is there a false sense of security, thinking that a personal experience is an answer to major questions in life? Is this *state of mind*, this *peace of mind*, which is the quest, maybe the goal of these searchers and practitioners, the right road to follow? It's up to you to answer this question.

Below you'll find some recent news articles about the *mind* related to *Audit of the Universe*. They give you an overall light into what *mind* is and how humankind is treating this critical issue:

The Sounds of Silence http://buff.ly/2r3cBEe The realization that whatever goes on inside or outside our bodies affects the #mind. Are we just making *noise* about this understanding, or are we doing something to remedy it? #theExplanation #AuditMind

Physical Safety or Emotional Security? http://buff.ly/2taH0Cz[9] #Mental[10] #health[11] related to daily living has taken center stage in our quest for balanced lives. Why is the #mind[12] so central? And, first of all, what is the mind and its role? #theExplanation[13] #AuditBrainMind[14]

---

8. http://www.ayahuasca-info.com/introduction

9. http://theexplanation.com/social-media-hashtags-comprising-the-coherent-completeness-of-the-universe/

10. https://www.facebook.com/hashtag/Mental

11. https://www.facebook.com/hashtag/health

12. https://www.facebook.com/hashtag/mind

Brain images display the beauty and complexity of #consciousness
http://buff.ly/2sXbjwv Extremely intricate; these images *only* display
little parts of the brain. It's impossible to imagine the complexity of all
these *pieces* working together instantaneously and continually to over-
see the life of each one of us. I'm not sure whether *consciousness* is the
right choice of words here. These images show functioning parts of the
#brain awareness. Can you scan #mind, memories? #theExplanation
#Auditbrainmind

Genes, Ions, and Other New Frontiers in Psychiatry http://buff.ly/
2tXjuvj This article is complex. Still, a rapid perusal by the uninitiated
reveals that dealing with the disorders of the #brain and mind #are not
easy. One of the key questions is: can brain #medication fix the mind?
A more fundamental question is: What's the difference between the
brain and the mind? #theExplanation #AuditBrainMind

Gunman Who Shot GOP Congressman Was a *Loner* http://buff.ly/
2sdPysE It's not the outer appearance of any individual that counts,
it's the inner-being. Former Alexandria Mayor Bill Euille, who chatted
with Hodgkinson at the gym, said, "I never saw him get mad when people were talking good, bad or ugly about any of the #political[15] par-
ties." Euille told The Associated Press. "He was just a very calm, rational
person, I thought." The inner-being is the #mind[16]; what are we doing
to help people's minds be respectable and decent? #theExplanation[17]
#Auditmind

---

13. https://www.facebook.com/hashtag/theexplanation

14. https://www.facebook.com/hashtag/auditBrainAndMind

15. https://www.facebook.com/hashtag/political

16. https://www.facebook.com/hashtag/mind

17. https://www.facebook.com/hashtag/theexplanation

Why do we need to get better at critiquing psychiatric diagnosis?
https://buff.ly/2yoYkWq Very complicated article about diagnosing
all types of #mental #disorders. Major point: Biological tests are relevant, but they EXCLUDE other causes. Physical, measurable #med-
ical #tests assure #psychiatrists that a BODILY function is not causing
the MENTAL disorder. Mental disorders are of the #MIND, and you
cannot physically test the mind. You can test the #BRAIN because it
is physical, but the mind is MENTAL and intangible. #theExplanation
#AuditMind

This Woman Saved the Americas From the Nazis https://buff.ly/
2y71aBX Amazing #woman, amazing untold story about #decoding,
amazing mind. Over decades of practice, Elizabeth solved tens of thousands of messages every year; she developed an #intuition, a way of
#thinking that made her one of the best in the #world at seeing the
shapes of #words in a field of #letters that nobody else could make sense
of. I classified this article under #AuditMind because it reveals what the
#human #mind is capable of. Nobody knows why. #theExplanation

What would you say the state of mind is on our planet? In the next
chapter, we'll take a closer look at the effects of violence and pornography on the mind.

The Mind, Affected by Violence and Sex

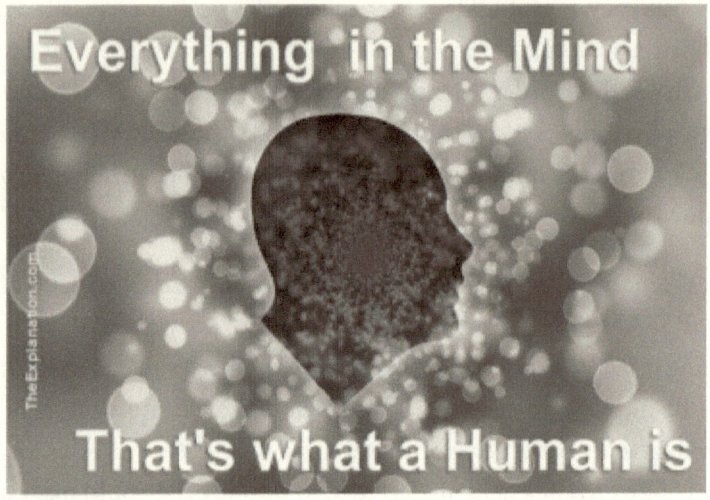

In the Mind, whether we realize it or not, each of us is being affected by the perverted violence and sex that pervades media.

In the mind resides everything that each human being has accumulated throughout their lifetime—all their experiences, ideas, memories, motivations, emotions, and feelings. **The mind not only summarizes what a human being is, but it also identifies each of us as an individual.**

In the last chapter, we discussed mental health and illnesses for which we can create and analyze statistics. Here, we are going to go a step further into an area that is more controversial where there are no statistics, where there's a lot of debate and disagreement: **The influence of *nurture on the mind.*** What I mean by nurture is the social environment in which each of us bathes.

What are some of the **very open and readily available practices in society that have an impact on our minds?** Violence (this is not just murders; it goes all the way from verbal abuse to harassment to violent cartoons and movies), sex, and drugs. I know that as soon as I write *violent cartoons,* some may think I'm old school. Listen to what the American Academy of Pediatrics has to say[1], "Extensive research evidence indicates that **media violence can contribute to aggressive behavior**, desensitization to violence, nightmares, and fear of being harmed."

We are talking about the **invisible impact of standard practices our minds are all exposed to,** day-in, day-out. Nowadays, you almost have to be a hermit to avoid the stream of news and especially vivid images hitting us via smartphone, TV, Twitter, FB, Instagram... The movie rating systems are very permeable as to what can be seen by under 10-13 year-olds.

The last two chapters, as well as the next book, *Audit of Humankind*, **focus specifically on the mind. What it is and the role it plays in human beings**. I remind you that I wrote **the mind is THE most critical element possessed by each of us**[2]. In theory, if you owned something costly and precious, like a jewel, house, or car, you'd want to pay extra attention to taking care of and protecting it.

One would think the same principle should apply to your mind, all of our minds. Are we doing this? Is society assuming its role as protertor? Is the half-filled glass getting emptier or fuller when it comes to caring for our minds? What follows is intended for one purpose only: To measure the influence that affects the state of our minds.

Shoot 'Em Up: Violent Video Games

---

1. https://www.livestrong.com/article/221006-how-tv-violence-affects-kids/

2. **http://theexplanation.com/mankinds-mind-the-key-to-final-notions-and-ideas-for-thought/**

In Newtown, Connecticut, USA, and Kauhajoki, Finland, an ocean apart, horrific scenes unfold before our eyes on the world stage, scenes of violence: schoolchildren and teachers shot to death in an American elementary school, and college students murdered in a Finnish vocational college. As police investigate the separate respective crimes, gunmen Adam Lanza and Matti Saari (who was friends with another mass shooter) have a **common link: they both played violent video games in the months and years leading up to their rampages.** Another violent offender (Devin Jones) who also plays video games tells police without emotion that **"life is like a video game."**

Matti Saari played the online virtual war multiplayer game "Battlefield 2," while Adam Lanza preferred Call of Duty, a first-person and third-person *shooter* game. Since the introduction of "Mortal Kombat," which features a martial arts expert demolishing his opponent, chopping a body in half and releasing a fountain of blood where the torso used to be. The video game cheerfully announces, "Fatality," and in a later fight with a female opponent, "Finish Her." All of these games, available for purchase and download and on Internet platforms, have a worldwide reach—and even more pertinent personal reach into the mind.

There are more *positive* games such as Lumosity.com[3], which uses proven neuroscience and learning methods to offer shape-matching, name-remembering, space-junk-clearing games that do contribute to healthier, more active brain function and increase brain plasticity. **Some people can find meaning in video games**—take the example of a 72-year-old man in England who, after the death of his wife and other horrible losses, begins playing an interactive game about aliens and recovers the will to live. It can be said that this 72-year-old man has more wisdom than a teenager and a more stable brain. Or perhaps the game he chooses is more uplifting than violent.

---

3. https://www.lumosity.com/

According to research, violent video games are entirely different[4], despite the game creators' protests and media's objections to the contrary, including one TV show's attempt to make a *nonviolent* video game that is utterly boring and has none of the swordplay/gunplay. Sword-clashing, killing multiple enemies, *powering up,* or choosing more and more exotic and destructive weapons. **The more *thoughts* in the mind of killing that already vulnerable teenager** or college students engage in, the more ideas of killing they will think, and the more those impulses can lead to action if not checked[5].

Video game characters resemble real people—the realism has increased over time. Lost in these electronic worlds, **children become *desensitized* to violence while at the same time *encouraged* to kill because of the nature of thoughts shaping in their minds.** Engaging in this play are several video gamers from South Korea, who can participate nonstop for over 50 hours at home or Internet Gaming Cafes. They shoot it out with "Starcraft," "Manhunt," or "Quake," the first game released in which players, 24/7, day and night, actually compete to virtually mow down other humans via their monster avatars by shooting them in the face.

One video game character in "Fable" intones to the heroes of the game, **"Your choices, whether they lead you down the path of good or evil, will change the face of the world."** In other words, will the players *choose* aggression or non-violence in the game? Will their *violent or peaceful choices* which are made in the mind, shape and encourage more aggressive play and greater desire to lose themselves in the fantasy world, of a boxing game, a war game, a sword-and-orc game?

---

4. https://edition.cnn.com/2016/07/25/health/video-games-and-violence/index.html

5. https://my.vanderbilt.edu/developmentalpsychologyblog/2014/04/effect-of-video-games-on-child-development/

People talk about video game *addiction*, but there can be no doubt there are even more powerful *just once* experiences that instantly change the brain and profoundly affect what's in the mind.

Pornography of the Mind

The success of the bestselling **Fifty Shades trilogy indicates that pornography and sadomasochism have gone mainstream**. Millions are reading a book, written by a woman, featuring intense scenes, associating sexuality with pain and domination, fusing two primal drives: sex and aggression.

The mass availability of video—online and offline—engraves images in the mind of men and women. We have no sense of the extent that our minds are being reshaped. Men and women have increasing difficulty being turned on by the opposite sex. They're interested in *fucking*, not making love, but they increasingly experience sexual dysfunctions. Because of pornography, they build up a tolerance to sexual excitement in the mind.

Their minds change because of what they have viewed. Pornography is all-pervasive; children can even access it on the Xbox during their *critical periods* of socializing. Parents are unaware that Google searches for pornography increase 4700% when children return from school or stay at home[6]. Estimates indicate that only 17% of teenage girls and 3% of boys have never watched pornography online. One billion (1,000,000,000) videos are being watched worldwide every single day[7] on the primary pornography websites and, as one former porn-star wrote, "whatever you do, your kids will inevitably see pornography."

---

6. https://www.netnanny.com/blog/pornography-searches-increase-4700-when-kids-are-out-of-school/

7. http://www.lepoint.fr/societe/ovidie-quoi-que-vous-fassiez-vos-enfants-verront-du-porno-23-02-2018-2197238_23.php

A very recent **inquiry in France revealed that sexual violence affects "all aspects of French society."**[8] The figures are massive: 58% of women say they have been victims of inappropriate behavior, 50% of insults or remarks of a sexist nature, 45% of gross gestures with a sexual connotation. Caresses or sexual touching without their consent affected 43% of women, 29% received pornographic messages by email or SMS, and finally, 12% endured one or more rapes.

I intend to demonstrate that **pornography and related sexual practices do profoundly impact what's in the mind.** The statistics for France are devastating. I don't know what they are for other countries, but when we have to consider women-only train coaches, spas, fitness centers[9], travel, etc. in certain countries, then we should understand that something is awry with the portrayal of sex.

We don't, and certainly won't, live in seclusion, free of internet, violence, and sex. But it's wise to be aware of the contrast of such living, with both a positive physical and mental life and the results it has on the body and mind.

The Famous Nun Study

8. https://www.francetvinfo.fr/societe/droits-des-femmes/info-franceinfo-violences-sex-uelles-12-des-femmes-ont-deja-subi-un-viol-selon-un-sondage_2621584.html#xtor_43ec3e5dee6e706af7766ff-fea512721_AL-79-_0bcef9c45bd8a48eda1b26eb0c61c869_5Barti-cle_0bcef9c45bd8a48eda1b26eb0c61c869_5D-_0bcef9c45bd8a48eda1b26eb0c61c869_5Bcon-nexe_0bcef9c45bd8a48eda1b26eb0c61c869_5D

9. https://www.self.com/story/i-worked-out-at-a-women-only-gym-to-see-if-id-feel-more-com-fortable

Sister Nicolette, one of 638 nuns from the School Sisters of Notre Dame, is 101 years old and still using her mind, most recently to help researchers understand Alzheimer's Disease[10]. This study is striking not only because of the nuns themselves but because of the power of the minds of the researchers, who have the insight to see that the sisters are living long, active, mentally healthy lives, well into their 90s and 100s. Committed to learning and service, Sister Nicolette and her fellow nuns have quite literally donated their brains to science. What's in their minds?

Galacti remarks, "Wow, the study publicity has it right: you would never imagine a convent could be a medical, neurological lab, yet it is."

Unlike traditional research, the Nun Study doesn't take place solely in the imaging lab, like in chapter 9 of *Inventory of the Universe*[11]. The original study author personally interacted and spent time with Sister Nicolette and the other study participants in their chapter homes and while they went about their life's work. In that sense, the study founder was exercising his own neuroplasticity by challenging his brain!

These sisters have an array of characteristics desired by the study authors: **No smoking, no drinking, same diet, same health care, same life circumstances, single throughout life, no children.** Also, from early childhood, they engaged in learning and ate a natural diet without all the processed foods of today's culture. Early childhood influences are *critical* in preventing/predicting Alzheimer's and other brain disorders. Also, **being busy and active later in life,** such as playing cards together and fiercely competing, volunteering, continuing to study, even showing *mad skills* in knitting little teddy bears as one sister does, helps build new neural networks throughout life even as the old connections are pruned away.

---

10. http://content.time.com/time/world/article/0,8599,2047984,00.html

11. http://theexplanation.com/the-brain-amazingly-small-amazingly-powerful-why/

You need both: a sound body and a sound mind, the physical and the non-physical, the bodily and the mental sides of each human being to have coherent completeness in understanding who and what a human being is. And you have to **treat each of those two elements correctly to have a sound body and sound mind.**

The Mind-Body Dilemma. Unsolved. Why?

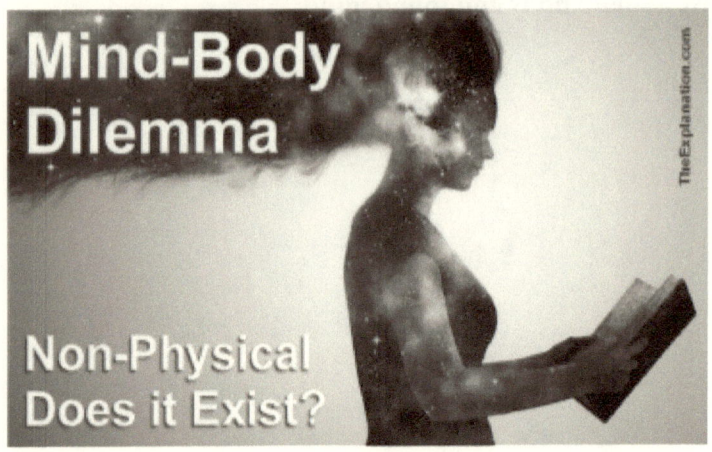

The Mind-Body issue is fundamental to what humans are. We know we have a body and mental capacities. But what is the relationship between the two? Mystery.

When it comes to human beings, the mind is the sole element setting us apart from animals.

The key to understanding *the Explanation* is the human mind. Let me say it clearly if you don't comprehend what the mind is and especially WHY each human being has a mind; you'll never get to first base.

I will also state at the end of this chapter, what the mind is. You won't get the reasons for my affirmations, not because I don't want to but because it's too early—first, the foundation. The rationale and answers are in the book *Origin of Humankind*. However, you will see, and I will point it out regularly in the next book, *Audit of Humankind,* that **without *mind* humankind and those chapters would not exist. The human mind, and ONLY the human mind makes possible:**

1. The Singularity of Humankind[1] (section 1 of the book *Audit of Humankind*
2. **How Humans Function** (section 2) ... read the first chapter here[2]
3. How Humans Socialize[3] (sec. 3) Humans have social relations because they have a mind
4. How Human Rule[4] (sec. 4) Humans work and accomplish only because of their mental capacities
5. How Humans Reason[5] (sec. 5) Humans espouse science, philosophy, and religion because they possess cognition

The human mind is the basis of ALL the above. Without the mind, the cognitive, we're just like upright standing apes and baboons. It behooves us to know what the *mind* is. Furthermore, it would be helpful to know WHY we have a mind, why each human being that has ever walked the face of this Earth has had a mind. **Whether we agree on what the mind is, we all have to admit that the mind is the *center of interest* of humankind.**

So, let me say that **humanity is in total confusion as to what the mind is.**

---

1. http://theexplanation.com/20_mans-singularity-dual-nature/

2. https://theexplanation.com/focus-on-human-behavior-study-how-humans-function/

3. https://theexplanation.com/human-society-the-only-global-social-species/

4. https://theexplanation.com/human-government-personal-world-peace/

5. https://theexplanation.com/reasoning-ability-logical-reasoning/

As with the body, you're going to hear a lot of conflicting information about the mind[6]; in fact, it's the same dilemma—are the body and the mind the same? In other words, are they both *physical*—one unit, in two electro-chemical parts? **Entire university programs are devoted to studying Computation Cognitive Neuroscience**[7]

> Understanding the relationship between brain, cognition, and behavior is one of the biggest challenges the scientific community is currently working on. Computational cognitive neuroscience is a young and exciting discipline that tackles these long-standing research questions by integrating computer modeling with experimental research.

> - Creating computational/mathematical models of neurons, circuits, and cognitive functions
> - The fundamentals of cognitive neuroscience (brain mechanisms and structures underlying cognition and behavior)
> - Advanced data analysis and neuroimaging techniques

Notice what's explicitly stated here: "**brain mechanisms and structures underlying cognition and behavior.**" Let's be clear. This presentation indicates that **the ORIGIN of cognition** ('the mental action or process of acquiring knowledge and understanding through thought, experience, and the senses') **and behavior is brain mechanisms and structures. The brain is the originator of the mind that leads to behavior**.

---

6. http://theexplanation.com/body-and-mind-are-the-brain-heart-and-gut-all-body-organs-the-mind/

7. https://www.gold.ac.uk/pg/msc-computational-cognitive-neuroscience

I have thrown you into the middle of one of the hottest debates that has been going on since the 17th century when Rene Descartes first pointed out the problem:

Mind-body dualism, or mind-body duality[8], is a view in the philosophy of mind that **mental phenomena are, in some respects, non-physical, or that the mind-body are distinct and separable.** Thus, it encompasses a set of views about the relationship between mind and matter, between subject and object, and is contrasted with other positions, such as physicalism and enactivism, in the mind-body problem

Today we call this the *body-mind dilemma*. There are shelves of books and material[9] on this subject and absolutely NO consensus whatsoever either in the world of scientists or philosophers. What I'm saying is this: **The greatest intellectual minds for the last 400 years have not reached a definitive conclusion as to what the *mind*—the mental, the human thinking process—truly is.**

Four hundred years, yet, did you notice the description of the university program above, "Computational cognitive neuroscience is a **young** and exciting discipline." In essence, this is a new twist on an age-old problem. And, some would say I'm repetitive, even paranoid, I'll just say for clarity sake, here's a definition of neuroscience:

Neuroscience (or neurobiology) is the scientific study of the nervous system[10]. It is a multidisciplinary branch of biology that deals with the anatomy, biochemistry, molecular biology, and physiology of neurons and neural circuits.

---

8. https://en.wikipedia.org/wiki/Mind%E2%80%93body_dualism

9. https://www.closertotruth.com/series/consciousness-entirely-physical

10. https://en.wikipedia.org/wiki/Neuroscience

Click on the link in that definition and read a little further. Do a little research yourself as to what *neuroscience* and *cognitive neuroscience* are. In my opinion, these disciplines are lopsided studies that start from the *truth* that the *mind* is an integral part of the *body*. Mind-body are one-and-the-same, so they say.

Yet, **no one has definitively solved this controversy**. And therein lies a severe difficulty.

Ask yourself a simple question: **How can you treat or cure someone who is sick if you don't even know what the base of the illness is?** How can you deal with mental sickness if you don't even know what the mind is? I'm not saying you can't help in such a situation. Many people have and are devoting their lives to do their utmost, and I salute them. All I'm doing is exposing the fundamentals of what many are taking for granted.

In this chapter, I want to help you understand one thing very clearly: the body-mind dilemma.

John Horgan is both an erudite and thorough journalist on the topic of Science. In my opinion, he has written some of the most unbiased material presenting both sides of this admittedly hard-to-understand problem. Here's an excerpt from an article he wrote regarding the body-mind issue[11]:

> **How does matter make mind? More specifically, how does a physical object generate subjective experiences** like those you are immersed in as you read this sentence? How does stuff become *conscious*? This is called the mind-body problem, or, by philosopher David Chalmers, the "hard problem."

---

11. https://blogs.scientificamerican.com/cross-check/can-integrated-information-theory-explain-consciousness/

I expressed doubt that the hard problem can be solved—a position called *mysterianism*—in *The End of Science*. I argue in a new edition[12] that my pessimism has been justified by the recent popularity of *panpsychism*. This ancient doctrine holds that consciousness is a property not just of brains but of *all* matter, like my table and coffee mug.

Panpsychism strikes me as self-evidently foolish, but non-foolish people—notably Chalmers and neuroscientist Christof Koch—are taking it seriously. How can that be? What's compelling their interest? Have I dismissed panpsychism too hastily?

Can you see the controversy here?

Neuroscience and Cognition take on all sorts of ideas and *names*. Below it's called 'Integrated information Theory'[13]. And here's what Physicist Marcelo Gleiser, interviewed by John Horgan, has to say about that[14].

> **Horgan:** Are you a fan of the new theory of consciousness, integrated information theory?

> **Gleiser:** I think a "fan" would be too strong a word, but I applaud Tononi and collaborators for trying to come up with a quantitative way of making sense of consciousness. Of course, the essential premise of IIT is that **consciousness is fundamental, sort of like as fundamental as space and time** (assuming these two are fundamental, another story al-

---

12. https://blogs.scientificamerican.com/cross-check/was-i-wrong-about-8220-the-end-of-science-8221/

13. https://en.wikipedia.org/wiki/Integrated_information_theory

14. https://blogs.scientificamerican.com/cross-check/the-more-we-know-the-more-mystery-there-is/

together). I find it hard to understand what that even means, as it focuses on ontology, what is real and what is not. I am more of a science-as-a-descriptive-tool kind of person, and **see consciousness in a more pragmatic and less fundamental way, as an emergent property of very complex neuronal patterns**. Of course, I could be wrong and we may indeed need a very new perspective on the nature of consciousness. Even so, I don't think making it just a mathematical theory will be enough. As with the origin of the universe, **the nature of human consciousness may be the kind of question that we may not be well-equipped to answer fully through a scientific approach**, even if we are able to artificially create some kind of limited consciousness through AI. This doesn't mean that consciousness has anything to do with supernaturalism; it simply means that some questions are not well-posed for our current scientific framework.

Again, **just notice the ambiguity in this reply**. Gleiser sees consciousness emerging from *complex neuronal patterns*. In other words, *body* and *mind* are one. He goes on to say that science may not be equipped to offer an answer to this problem, and then, although he brings up supernaturalism (the non-physical), he brushes that aside by saying we're not asking the right questions. Amazing pirouette. The mind-body issue is a puzzle.

Here's a link to Tim Crane and Sarah Patterson's work: History of the Mind-Body Problem[15]. On page 169, they point out what I'm stating in this chapter:

---

15. http://14.139.206.50:8080/jspui/bitstream/1/1779/1/Crane&Patterson%20(ed.)%20-%20History%20of%20the%20Mind-Body%20Problem.pdf

"...leaves contemporary philosophers with their problem: **mental causation inclines them towards physicalism, while consciousness inclines them towards dualism.**"

I realize there's difficult vocabulary here. It is saying that the *mental* is caused by the physical (only) whereas conscience is dual, that is, contains both physical and non-physical phenomena.

If you read some of their work and any other works on the subject of mind-body, you will see two camps.

1. One camp believes that **everything, mind, mental, conscience, etc. is PHYSICAL.** In other words has solely to do with the body, cells, synapses, neurons, and neuronal networks. This approach is monism. ONE source.
2. The other camp leans towards **dualism. TWO sources. The first being the physical body, the second being something *outside* the body**—whatever that *something* might be.

Since the scientific world cannot use words like *spiritual* or even *supernaturalism* (which Gleiser used above), hence the creation of erudite terms like *raw feels, sensa, phenomenal qualities, intrinsic properties of conscious experiences,* the *qualitative content of mental states,* and probably the best-known *qualia.* A general, more understandable term used here is *non-physical.* I shall define this *non-physical* in more detail.

On a lighter concluding note, last night I watched a TV documentary about the saga of Tupperware. Quite a story. At one point, the commentator said, "In the USA there was a shortage of raw materials, and only the human mind could come up with synthesizing a product to replace the natural, in this case, using the residue of petroleum to create malleable plastic." It's the story of Earl Tupper[16]. I leave you with the thought: **Is it the physical human brain and neural networks that can imagine, synthesize, and create?**

The investigation will be continued.

---

16. https://en.wikipedia.org/wiki/Earl_Tupper

Artificial Intelligence and Transhumanism

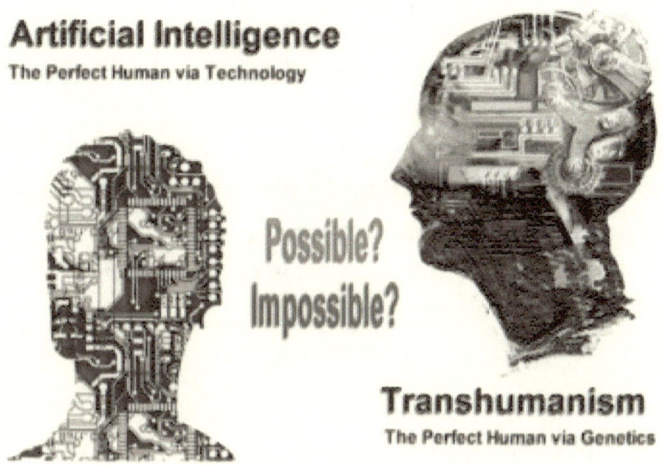

Artificial Intelligence
The Perfect Human via Technology

Possible?
Impossible?

Transhumanism
The Perfect Human via Genetics

Artificial Intelligence and transhumanism are the buzz-words now promising a brighter future. Intelligence in machines and genetics that exhibits behavior and reactions like super-humans.

Artificial intelligence is the equivalent of *creating the mind of a human.* That's what science has to accomplish. Then we've got to associate that artificial mind with a perfected human body. Science is developing that improved human body as I write this chapter. This discipline is known as *transhumanism.*

The definition of transhumanism is a way of thinking that advocates the use of science and technology to improve the physical and mental characteristics of humans[1]. The basis for this approach is the concept

---

1. https://iatranshumanisme.com/transhumanisme/

that humans are currently in the middle phase of development. Indeed, the *transhuman* corresponds to a state that is between the *human* and the *post-human*. The post-human will have **abilities far beyond those of today's humans** and, therefore, would not be considered a *human* according to our current standards.

For example, this post-human would be **resistant to illness**, have eternal youth, control over desires, moods, and mental states. Post-human would not be prone to **feel fatigue, hatred, or stress** as well as having an excellen**t capacity for feelings of pleasure, love, appreciation of art, and serenity**. In fact, s/he could experience new states of consciousness that the **current human brain can not reach**.

Wow, I can't wait.

Science and technology, in all their splendor and forms, are devoting much effort to create *wonder-humans*. Let me break it down for you in understandable terms.

In the last chapter, we discussed the body-mind dilemma: What's the body? What's the mind? And primarily how the two interact. We understand that these questions are 400 years old, and **in 2020 there is NON CONSENSUS on the nature of *mind* and, above all, how it works with the body.** Interaction is a total enigma. Transhumanism and Artificial Intelligence are just the modern versions, with hyped-up vocabulary, of this age-old dilemma.

Body = Transhumanism

Mind = Artificial Intelligence

We are **to believe that not only has the body-mind issue been solved, BUT that science and technology can build a superior body-mind human.** What do you think about that?

I'm certainly not an expert on either artificial intelligence or transhumanism. So I'm passing it over to John Horgan via quotes from his book *Undiscovered Mind*.[2] He's interviewed many of the fathers and experts in these fields. Here are some choice pieces of what he has to say (page numbers are in brackets):

- A common problem in describing human mental life, the theory of mind, is the notion that the mind is divided into modules dedicated to specific tasks. These assumptions are limited, but it still leaves unanswered the question of how the results of all these modular computations become integrated (page 197).
- "Common sense is egregiously what the computers that we know how to build don't have." Horgan concludes: "Evolutionary psychology and AI are both bumping up against the Humpty Dumpty dilemma. They can break the mind into pieces, but they have no idea how to put it back together again (198).

Not even the most avid artificial intelligence enthusiast claims that these programs represent a serious challenge to human composers, artists and poets (205).

- In 1997 the computer Deep Blue defeated Gary Kasparov, examining 200 million chess positions per second. Deep Blue succeeds NOT by trying to mimic human judgment but by reducing the problem to pure computation. The techniques that tried to mimic human judgment failed miserably. Joseph Hoane (principal software engineer for the Deep Blue project) concurred. "We still don't know how to do that at all." (207).

---

2. https://www.amazon.com/Undiscovered-Mind-Replication-Medication-Explanation/dp/0684865785

- Thinking is a very difficult word. The brain is more than hardware. It's all the software and everything else. (208).
- A network can be *trained* to recognize patterns with greater accuracy. Neural networks acquire knowledge. But, in practice, neural networks have turned out to be as limited and inflexible as rule-based methods. Horgan doubts the rule-based network will lead to truly intelligent machines (209).
- Human intelligence has the capacity for rapidly processing and acting on ambiguous, open-ended data, to draw on a vast reservoir of worldly knowledge that might be called common sense (211).
- Neural networks have the same problem as AI: an inability to duplicate common sense. There's been no progress in understanding the mind (213).
- In domains such as language understanding and common sense, which are basically limitless in their possibilities and hard to specify, we fall far short. AI so far has been a failure (214).
- The goal of building truly intelligent machines had not been achieved (219).
- Neural networks are trying to understand biological systems... we're overlooking some vital component (222).
- We've failed to do justice to the mind's complexity. Mind-scientists and philosophers cannot even agree on what CONSCIOUSNESS is let alone how it should be explained (228).

That's quite an indictment of artificial intelligence and transhumanism. Don't get me wrong. We are making and will make great strides in genetics and perfecting machines and trying to get them to act more and more like human beings. Indeed there are *nurse, reception-*

ist, and *baby-sitting* machine-robots. We will make progress, but **they will be programmed machines unendowed with the capacity of the human mind.**

Because we don't understand the critical place and role the mind plays in human beings, **we go awry in putting great belief in the capacities of science and medicine** to produce super-humans.

Let me be open. You'll need to understand the overall concept I'm going to develop here.

Historically, **until the end of the 1800's the religious concept that the mind was a non-physical entity, dualism (body+mind=2) reigned.** From the 20th century onward, **the monistic (body+mind=1) viewpoint has gradually but steadily made headway to where nowadays it is practically presented as FACT.** The mind is an integral, inseparable part of the brain.

The result of this amalgamation causes science to reduce everything to *treating the brain, including the mind, as part of the body.* This basis is the whole quest of genetics—find the *genetics* of everything, manipulate the genes that control alcohol, sex, anger—and boom—we'll have better humanity. That is the ultimate goal of transhumanism. The belief or theory that the human race can evolve beyond its current physical and mental limitations, primarily through science.

Artificial Intelligence is working from the other end of the spectrum. They have already concluded that *human is physical* (the mind is physical), so they can build a PHYSICAL MACHINE that will be HUMAN.

The basis of this one concept alone is the MIND is PHYSICAL.

IF the mind is NON-physical, then both Transhumanism and Artificial Intelligence are bunk, and the proponents of these concepts are barking up the wrong tree.

In the next book, *Audit of Humankind*[3], I will show why **this vagrant vision of the future of humanity is not viable.** In the book *Origin of Humankind*[4], I will show you **a viable alternative to Transhumanism and Artificial Intelligence.**

Please retain the key from this chapter; it's **up to you to decide:** Whether the MIND is a PHYSICAL integral part of the BRAIN and GENETICS or whether it is a NON-PHYSICAL entity that totally escapes the body and is an entity of and by itself that we need to treat as such.

---

3. *https://theexplanation.com/read-all-the-content-of-audit-of-humankind-online/*

4. *https://theexplanation.com/read-content-origin-humankind-online/*

Consciousness and the Human Mind

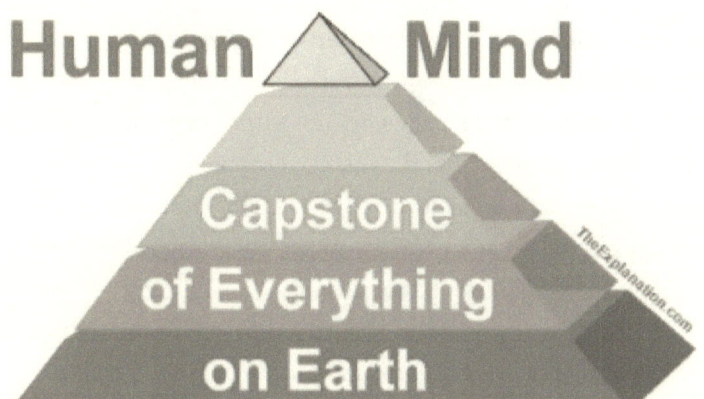

Consciousness goes hand in hand with the human mind. Understand the one, and you'll understand the other. Hey, did you realize that the only way to understand is via consciousness and the human mind!

Consciousness, together with the human mind, are among the greatest enigmas of all times. Yet, they are the basis and key to understanding humankind. Why you are, who you are. And beyond that, why each of us has a human mind and consciousness. Embark on *The Explanation* and learn why.

As this is *Audit of the Universe,* **we have discussed the state of the human mind** and mental health. However, **we are also defining the final pieces and contours of our puzzle so we can begin to put it together in *Origin of the Universe*.** After all, if you don't have the parts or have the wrong pieces, you'll never be able to assemble it and display the co-herent and complete image, correct? You must establish a solid foundation before constructing the building and roof.

Here's a principle for building anything solidly. An example from a different field: In search engine optimization, we call these **critical pieces of a website, cornerstone pages**, the essential pages for which all the other pages give more precise details, the cornerstone knowledge from which all the other information pages branch out. Before you start, you've got to know what those first pages are going to be. And you've got to know the single overriding idea, the raison d'être for your website. That's the capstone page, at the very top, which the limited number of cornerstone pages, on the second level, begin to expand... and so on with more detailed pages at the third and fourth levels.

Same with *The Explanation*. **We must establish the lead element, the top-ranking feature from which the four cornerstone elements** derive. It's like starting at the top of a pyramid, as you can see from the image above. We're talking about the pyramidion, the capstone. The second row from the top contains the four cornerstones, and along with all the other layers of stones, they support this one top-level jewel. **The crowning stone that all the others develop and point to**.

> **For the universe and humankind, the capstone is the human mind.**

We have analyzed the body-mind issue[1] with monism and dualism. We have referred to Transhumanism and Artificial Intelligence[2] as proposed for progressing to the next level of *super-humans*. I've displayed

---

1. http://theexplanation.com/the-mind-body-dilemma-400-years-old-and-still-unsolved-why/

2. http://theexplanation.com/the-illusion-of-artificial-intelligence-and-transhumanism/

lists of hundreds of emotions, attitudes, sentiments, and moods[3] and asked you where we can find them? Are they in robots? Computers? And especially, are they part of the human body and brain?

Dr. Lieff MD blogged about this for several years: Searching for the Mind[4]. He is now writing a book on cellular intelligence. On his blog, he wrote a post entitled, **Where is Subjective Experience in the Brain?**. Subjective means personal, internal, emotional gut reaction. Here's what he wrote on May 1, 2016[5]:

> "Current science has no explanation for subjective experience. There isn't even an adequate definition of consciousness. Recent research continues many approaches in attempts to find a brain region that is correlated with basic awareness or consciousness."

What I particularly appreciate about Dr. Lieff is his frankness about research and its accomplishments. **Subjective experience is directly associated with the mind. If there's no explanation for the former, then there's no explanation for the latter.** He admits that science and research are at a loss to define consciousness. I'm not criticizing either science or medicine or research; I just want you to beware and be very careful when you hear affirmations that say it's part of the brain, which implies the mind is physical.

Dr. Lieff concludes his article with:

> "There is still no understanding of how subjective experience binds together all that is part of our daily experience of awareness. Most events in the brain involve large brain wide

3. http://theexplanation.com/the-human-mind-is-it-a-body-part-part-of-the-brain-or-somewhere-else/

4. http://jonlieffmd.com

5. http://jonlieffmd.com/blog/subjective-experience-brain

circuits traversed in milliseconds. Just this week, a study implied meaning of words is not in a language center, but distributed throughout the entire brain. The same is true for memory, which appears to be very distributed.

No brain region simply reflects consciousness. Some regions are correlated with content of awareness. For now, this search will continue with no definition of consciousness or subjective experience. We are left with our every day experience."

Please understand what I'm doing here. **We're discussing the individual components of a human being.** In *Inventory of the Universe* section 8[6] and the last section of *Audit of the Universe*[7]: **The body which should also include the brain, a vital body organ.** Whereas chapter 9 of both *Inventory*[8] and *Audit*[9] treat more with **the mind.** Yes, **I've separated the mind from the body** devoting chapter 9 in both volumes to this *separate or not to separate* issue.

Some readers might not see why I'm trying to drive home this point. And true, I won't be entirely clear until we get into *Origin of the Humankind* when I give you all the answers. **I've separated the mind from the body and brain and transhumanism and Artificial Intelligence because the mind is an elusive, but oh, so vital *part* of a human being.** The controversy that surrounds the body-mind issue should tell you how thorny this unsolved problem is.

---

6. http://theexplanation.com/category/read-inventory-of-the-universe-online/human-body/

7. http://theexplanation.com/category/read-audit-of-the-universe-online/8-audit-human-body/

8. http://theexplanation.com/category/read-inventory-of-the-universe-online/brain-mind/

9. *http://theexplanation.com/category/read-audit-of-the-universe-online/audit-brain-and-mind/*

You are going to see in the next book *Audit of Humankind*, what I could call the five cornerstones, that, **without mind, it would be impossible to write.** The *Singularity of Humankind.* **How Humankind Functions, Socializes, Rules, and Reasons.** Simply because **without the Human Mind, we'd function just like animals.**

In 2014 the biography of Stephen Hawking was released as a film: The Theory of Everything. Here's what Matthew Murray a managing editor at PC Magazine wrote[10],

> **"Technology is capable of helping us get anywhere,** verbalize any thought to any number of people. Each of us alive right now has far more resources than Hawking ever did, and can affect many more lives more easily than he could at the height of his physical powers.
>
> **But no computer, no device, will ever replace the one-of-a-kind tools within us,** which not only make us unique but also make us uniquely capable to participate in and re-shape the world around us. **It's from the human mind, not electronics, that our greatest ideas spring**, and it's through them that we move furthest ahead when we most need to.
>
> As *The Theory of Everything* demonstrates, Stephen Hawking has known that for decades. And despite the plethora of challenges he's faced, he's never slowed down. Neither should we, if we want to not only touch the stars, but understand them."

Matthew Murray is devoted to electronics (Managing editor of PC Magazine). Yet, he writes, **"It's from the human mind, not electronics, that our greatest ideas spring."** In his last paragraph of homage to

10. https://www.pcmag.com/article2/0,2817,2471808,00.asp

a great scientist, he recognizes that Hawking's life was a matter of *mind over body*. Hawking's mind kept him going, learning, discovering, writing, sharing knowledge. Those are all *mind* or *mental attributes*.

Psyche, this and that but everywhere

Psyche is Greek for soul or spirit. Whenever scientists or doctors use the words *psyche...* (psychosomatic, psychology, psychedelic, psychopath, psychosis), or *cognitive,* you can substitute the concept *mind*. If you think about how many fields incorporate these terms, you begin to realize the role the *mind* plays. Just how much information there is floating around out there about the *mind*.[11] And, in this profusion of information, a lot of confusion of concepts, proposals, and treatments.

We talked about the state of mental health. **Psyche incorporates phenomena that reach into the very depth of each human being.** Nothing is more profound than your and my feelings, attitudes, and emotions. Today, these manifestations of our psyche are often troubled as we refer to soul, spirit, (inner) self, innermost self, (inner) ego, true being, essential nature, life force, vital, force, inner man/woman, persona, identity, personality, individuality, make-up, subconscious, mind, intellect. All these terms are another way of talking about the psyche.

Incredible technology has developed increasingly precise mapping of the brain, and it will only get even better and more detailed. Yet we still only recognize which *regions* of the brain are responsible for individual functions. And we realize more and more, as Dr. Lieff mentioned above regarding language that **the brain acts as a whole.** But, we have not located or identified where a specific memory, like your first infatuation or the love of your pet, resides. Let alone where we can locate your moods of anger, jealousy, philanthropy, and sharing. **We can scan the brain; we can't scan the psyche.**

---

11. https://en.wikipedia.org/wiki/Psyche

Norman Doidge M.D. wrote in *The Brain that Changes Itself.*

> "Everything your "immaterial" mind imagines leaves materi-
> al traces. Each thought alters the physical state of your brain
> synapses."

This immaterial, this psyche, this subconscious, these moods are what
Descartes referred to,

> "when arguing that mind and brain are made of different
> substances and are governed by different laws. The brain,
> Descartes claimed, was a physical and material thing, exist-
> ing in space and obeying the laws of physics. The mind (or
> the soul, as he called it) was immaterial, a thinking thing that
> did not take up space or obey physical laws. Thoughts, he
> argued, were governed by the rules of reasoning, judgment,
> and desires, not by the physical laws of cause and effect. Hu-
> man beings consisted of this duality, this marriage of imma-
> terial mind and material brain.
>
> But Descartes—whose mind/body division has dominated
> science for four hundred years—could never credibly ex-
> plain how the immaterial mind could influence the material
> brain.
>
> But now we can see that our 'immaterial' thoughts too have
> a physical signature, and we cannot be so sure that thought
> won't someday be explained in physical terms. While we
> have yet to understand exactly *how* thoughts actually change
> brain structure, it is now clear that they do, and the firm line
> that Descartes drew between mind and brain is increasingly
> a dotted line." (excerpts from pages 213-214)

It is clear that "immaterial thoughts" leave material traces. **Somehow something from the yet to be fully defined impalpable cognitive, psyche, mind materially affects and leaves a measurable imprint on the physical brain.** We can see it happening via a scan and witness the neuronal modifications. John Horgan, in *The Undiscovered mind* on page 46, recognizes this schema:

> "Over the course of his career, Freud became increasingly skeptical about whether the mind could be explained in physiological (a branch of biology that deals with the functions living matter: organs, tissues, cells, neurons ... and of the physical and chemical phenomena involved) terms ... he seemed to rule out the possibility that psychology would ever be united with neuroscience. (Sam: the immaterial with the material, trying to ascertain how the *mind* works by delving into the *physical* and *chemical* structure).
>
> We know two things about the psyche (or mental life):
>
> Its bodily organs and scene of action: the brain or nervous system
>
> Our acts of consciousness, which are immediate data and cannot be further explained by any sort of description
>
> **Everything that lies in between is unknown to us**, and the **data do not include any direct relation between these two terminal points of our knowledge.** If it existed, it would at the most afford an exact localization of the processes of consciousness and would give us no further help toward understanding them."

John Horgan, Norman Doidge, and apparently Freud himself, knew that **the MENTAL acts on the PHYSICAL**. HOW and WHAT takes place—the process—is not visible to scientists: How the consciousness of emotions, reasoning, imagination, thoughts is transmitted to the material brain is an enigma. The same mystery that Descartes struggled with:

The interface between the mental and the physical is a question you practically never hear anything about. **If science can't define *mind* , how can it begin to decipher how the mind affects the body?** Let me try to put this in practical terms using the computer as an example. It's a good example because, although most of the population know what it is and use it, there's an element that few really understand.

There are three major elements to a computer, and you must have all three for it to be of any use to a user.

1. **Hardware-the machine**: keyboard/mouse for input, hard disk drive where the input/memory resides, screen for the output of the memory. A processor to accomplish the commands you give the computer and, of course, there are ears/microphone-speakers, eyes/video camera, mouth/printer, etc. There are a hardware handler and coordinator of all these components, and wouldn't you know that we call it the motherboard. Why not the father board?

2. **The operating system for the hardware:** It tells the hardware what to do when it's turned on, how to process and where to record data on the disks, how to recuperate it etc., We now have a touchscreen, it has to cause the machine to enact whatever your finger movement does. It makes sure all the hardware components integrate and complement each other.

3. **Application software for the human user:** These programs represent productivity—processing—software that allows you

and me to write and create letters, books... record sound and images, calculate, draw, design, present, develop databases, send messages, share. These processing applications allow each of us to express our creativity.

All three parts must work together perfectly, with no bugs. That's the goal of a computer.

Everyone knows there's hardware, the first element; they see the computer and screen; they turn it on and off. I view the production of my typing in the form of words or images which I create to introduce each blog post. **Concerning the application software—the third element—everyone learns and tries to become proficient** in writing, calculating, creating graphics and recording voice or gaming, using programs designed for those purposes.

But **many don't pay any attention to the second element, the operating system, the INTERFACE between machine and user**. Some barely know it even exists. Personally, when something goes wrong at that level, I'm at a loss. **The interface is a highly sophisticated program that must operate correctly so that the computer (1st element) seamlessly outputs what we key into (3rd element) the machine.**

Likewise, with the mind and the brain, the conscious and the body. **There has to be an interface between the mental and the physical.** This subject is much bigger and has far more impact than most of us begin to realize. It is **the crux of human existence**. This mind-body junction is what stumped Descartes. It stumps scientists and philosophers who put their minds (hmm ... *put their minds*) into thinking about this thorny issue.

There are a lot of blanks to be filled in: **We don't know what the mind and consciousness really are, and we don't comprehend the interface—the mechanism—that causes the mind to imprint on the**

physical. There's a lot of explaining to be done. And yet the mind and consciousness are the base of everything human. Do you see how fundamental this piece of the puzzle is?

Some questions to ponder:

- The mind is plastic; you can change your mind just as the body and brain are. But why is the mind plastic?
- Hands are what accomplish the thoughts of the mind. I think about the contents of this chapter and my hands type those thoughts on the keyboard, Why can only humans outwardly express not only their emotions, moods, and attitudes but also their creativity, ideas, and imagination, whatever is on their mind?

A final quote from John Horgan's Undiscovered Mind (page 253):

> "No account of the universe in its totality can be final which leaves these other forms of consciousness quite disregarded"

Horgan says you can't do an *Inventory* or an *Audit of the Universe* without all the pieces of the puzzle. And **consciousness, the essence of humankind is such a significant piece**; you cannot disregard it.

That is why I'm writing *The Explanation* series. We shall elaborate on this fundamental piece in *Audit of Humankind*. In *Origin of Humankind*, we'll see the origin of consciousness and mind, how they work, their raison d'être, and especially their relation to humankind. Consciousness and mind represent the capstone of everything in the Universe.

Epilogue

In the first book of The Explanation series, *Inventory of the Universe*, we surveyed our known environment to ascertain whether we had all the pieces of the puzzle.

The idea is to see how they are all integrated into a coherent, complete picture. Each piece has a role to play. Not only withdrawing a piece but also misplacing it throws the entire image out of focus.

Indeed, our Universe and, in particular, our planet Earth are marvelously assembled. Systems in systems in yet other systems. All are working together in just-in-time harmony to establish the most suitable environment for humankind.

We have just finished the second phase of making sense of our puzzle. We've analyzed its state. Like evaluating the livability of a house or the drivability of a car. We have completed an audit of Space, Atmosphere, Water, Land, Flora, Fauna, Life, and the Human Body and Mind to see their stability. And, especially to see whether the human presence, the most significant influence on Earth's welfare, is assuming its responsibility regarding its home.

It's up to you to decide how Earth is faring.

We're ready to plunge into the biggest enigma on this planet, ourselves.

The next book in *The Explanation* series, *Audit of Humankind*, places human beings under a microscope. Humankind is a species apart from everything else on Earth, and maybe in the Universe.

Whereas animals can function minutes after their birth, in a lot of cases, without the presence of either parent, human babies take years to grow to maturity. How do we explain the whole process of marriage and parenthood? There are so many notions specific to humans, like why do they have to work to earn a living? Why do they have to dress? Why do they cook their food? Animals do none of these. We shall see how they interrelate and their role in the puzzle

Audit of Humankind not only helps you evaluate what humankind is doing with their home planet, but it also goes deep inside the human mind to see how each of us ticks.

It covers vital subjects that need to be understood to grasp the 21st-century state of humankind.

- The Singularity of Humankind
- How Humankind Functions
- How Humankind Socializes
- How Humankind Rules
- How Humankind Reasons

In preparation for answers to the primary subjects of the *Origin of the Universe* and *Origin of Humankind,* we have to place the final, but most important, pieces of the puzzle on the table. Get ready to plunge into the depths of what humans and their minds really are. Let's complete our *Audit.*

References

All these links were active at time of publishing. Internet is dynamic, so if any are not clickable please let me know at sam@theexplanation.com. You can also send references, that corroborate the state of the Universe and Earth. I will look them over and eventually add them to the website and other media. Thanks.

Preface

Migratory birds crossing Sahara:

http://rsbl.royalsocietypublishing.org/content/early/2009/11/25/rsbl.2009.0785.full

Bird Sanctuary in Eilat: http://www.thesolutionsjournal.com/node/925

Mt Everest: https://phys.org/news/2018-06-mount-everest-high-altitude-rubbish-dump.html

Chapter 1 - Space

Web articles:

Korea nuclear test & earthquake: http://www.bbc.co.uk/news/world-asia-21421841

http://www.v2rocket.com/start/chapters/mittel.html

http://www.bbc.co.uk/history/british/empire_seapower/launch_ani_navigation.shtml

http://electronics.howstuffworks.com/gadgets/travel/gps.htm

http://www.universetoday.com/25145/interesting-facts-about-stars/

http://www.smartplanet.com/blog/bulletin/the-shortest-route-russia-ships-gas-to-japan-via-arctic/8553?tag=search-river

http://articles.timesofindia.indiatimes.com/2010-12-30/india/28252475_1_wheelers-island-agni-ii-brahmos-cruise-missile

http://spinoff.nasa.gov/Spinoff2004/hm_5.html

http://www.nasa.gov/topics/earth/features/india_water.html

Orbital debris: http://images.spaceref.com/news/2009/ODMedia-Briefing28Apr09-1.pdf

https://www.space.com/26078-how-many-stars-are-there.html

Articles:

Paul Davies, "Law and order in the Universe," New Scientist, October 15, 1998, p. 59.

Documentaries:

Pax American: the Militarization of Space, 2009

Chapter 2 - Atmosphere

Web articles:

http://www.universetoday.com/48328/earth-surface-temperature/#ixzz2DYYSmvsT

http://davidsbeenhere.com/2016/01/26/choosing-an-air-pollution-mask-for-china/

http://edition.cnn.com/2015/12/08/asia/china-pollution-artist/

http://www.stuff.co.nz/world/asia/8236408/Canned-air-for-sale-in-China-as-smog-returns

Pollution from ships: http://io9.com/5983698/ - http://www.nitrousoxide.org

Global Drought Information System[1]: http://www.drought.gov/gdm/current-conditions

Canadian Arctic green: http://pubs.aina.ucalgary.ca/arctic/Arctic5-3-134.pdf

Meningitis Vaccine Project: http://www.meningvax.org

Dust and Disease: https://www.theguardian.com/world/2009/sep/27/dust-storms-diseases-sydney

Lyme in NE states USA: http://www.foxnews.com/health/2017/03/13/lyme-disease-soars-in-michigan-as-tick-populations-grow.html

Biochar: https://permaculturenews.org/2010/11/18/beware-the-biochar-initiative/ https://www.cleancookingalliance.org/home/index.html

Aral Sea: http://www.eurasianet.org/node/65167

http://www.world-weather-travellers-guide.com/london-smog.html

http://scienceblog.com/42352/ice-cores-yield-rich-history-of-climate-change/#Z3EcRMYacipD8j6Z.99

http://www.carbonbrief.org

---

1. http://www.drought.gov/gdm/

http://www.guardian.co.uk/environment/interactive/2013/may/13/ newtok-alaska-climate-change-refugees

http://www.guardian.co.uk/world/2009/sep/27/dust-storms-diseases-sydney

Diarrhea linked to prolonged droughts in Africa: http://www.eenews.net/stories/1059978732

http://www.cleanerandgreener.org/resources/air-pollution.html

http://www.tropical-rainforest-animals.com/air-pollution-causes.html

https://timesofindia.indiatimes.com/city/chennai/Toxic-air-stunts-babies-growth/articleshow/18491353.cms

http://economix.blogs.nytimes.com/2013/06/28/the-myriad-benefits-of-a-carbon-tax/

http://www.mining.com/10000-mining-jobs-cut-in-australia-over-the-last-couple-of-months-57241/

http://www.csmonitor.com/Science/2013/0307/Global-temperature-rise-is-fastest-in-at-least-11-000-years-study-says

Documentaries/Videos:

ABC News Footage: http://abcnews.go.com/Archives/video/aug-2003-european-heat-wave-10487326

An Inconvenient Truth, 2005

Climate Refugees, 2009: http://www.climaterefugees.com

Chapter 3 - Water

Web articles:

Lake Chad: https://ourworld.unu.edu/en/sucking-dry-an-african-giant

https://www.nationalgeographic.com/photography/proof/2017/05/lake-chad-desertification/

http://www.upi.com/Business_News/Energy-Resources/2012/10/19/Egypt-pushes-Ethiopia-to-scrap-Nile-dam/UPI-74581350658245/

http://www.infowars.com/war-over-nile-river-water-between-egypt-and-ethiopia/

http://www.smh.com.au/business/japan-turns-back-to-coalfired-power-plants-20130425-2ihb0.html:

Wheat consumption in Israel in 2012: http://www.thecropsite.com/reports/?id=225&country=IL

http://www.occasionalplanet.org/2013/04/22/garbage-patch-nation/:

http://www.fws.gov/news/blog/index.cfm/2012/10/24/Discarded-plastics-distress-albatross-chicks:

https://www.indiegogo.com/projects/fontus-the-self-filling-water-bottles-sport-camping#/[2]

Waterboy: http://www.abs-cbnnews.com/lifestyle/07/26/13/machine-creates-water-air

---

2. https://www.indiegogo.com/projects/fontus-the-self-filling-water-bottles-sport-camping#_6666cd76f96956469e7be39d750cc7d9_

http://www.philstar.com/news-feature/2013/08/03/1045571/new-tech-makes-water-air

https://bottleschools.org/chapter-1/how-to-build-a-bottle-school/

Record of melting glaciers in 2012: http://www.maxisciences.com/fonte-des-glaces/fonte-des-glaces-les-chiffres-record-de-2012-alarment-l-039-onu_art29427.html

Varanasi funeral pyres: http://www.outlookindia.com/article.aspx?277355

http://www.popularmechanics.com/science/energy/hydropower-geothermal/will-himalayan-dams-solve-indias-energy-woes-14982175

Water sanitation: http://www.unicef.org/wash/files/2012_WASH_Annual_Report_14August2013_eversion_(1).pdf

Showering and water: http://www.dailymail.co.uk/news/article-2067020/Power-showers-garden-sprinklers-water-use—money-drain.html[3]

http://cleanwaterfortheworld.org

http://www.cdc.gov/healthywater/drinking/public/water_disinfection.html

Harnessing the Yellow River: http://europe.chinadaily.com.cn/china/2013-03/31/content_16361917.htm

Flood prediction for the Yellow River: http://www.chinadaily.com.cn/china/2012-05/16/content_15307851.htm

---

3. http://www.dailymail.co.uk/news/article-2067020/Power-showers-garden-sprinklers-water-use--money-drain.html

http://www.scientificamerican.com/article.cfm?id=does-china-have-enough-water-burn-coal:

http://phys.org/news/2013-06-otters-disease-rivers.html

http://neptune911.wordpress.com/2013/08/23/over-500-oceanic-dead-zones-counted/

Baltic Sea pollution: http://www.csmonitor.com/2003/0623/p07s01-woeu.html/(page)/2

http://www.upi.com/Business_News/Energy-Resources/2013/04/05/Russia-seeks-Baltic-pollution-partnerships/UPI-56841365134700/

http://yle.fi/uutiset/finnish_officials_polish_phosphorus_leakages_vast/6737747

Marine pharmacology: https://www.ncbi.nlm.nih.gov/pmc/articles/PMC4832911/

http://articles.latimes.com/2012/nov/20/local/la-me-water-deal-20121120

http://www.azcentral.com/story/news/local/arizona-environment/2017/09/27/u-s-and-mexico-agree-share-colorado-river-conservation-and-possible-shortage/710649001/

https://www.infowars.com/organic-from-china-exposed-the-shocking-truth-about-organic-foods-grown-in-the-worlds-worst-environmental-cesspool/

Documentaries/Videos:

Water Week 2012: http://www.worldwaterweek.org/sa/node.asp?node=1616

Water Wars, 2009

Running Dry: http://www.runningdry.org/world.html

Poisoned Waters, PBS: http://www.pbs.org/wgbh/pages/frontline/poisonedwaters/

Technology:

http://www.aquasciences.com/

Other Research:

Visit to Cambodia, June 28-29, 2011: Angkor Thom, Angkor Wat, Banteay Srei, Ta Prohm, Tonle Sap River, and Tonle Sap Lake

Visit to Borobudur Temple, Indonesia, July 12, 2011

Chapter 4 - Land

Vittel:

http://www.fao.org/fileadmin/user_upload/pes-project/docs/FAO_RPE-PES_Vittel-France.pdf

Quinoa: https://nacla.org/news/2018/03/12/quinoa-boom-goes-bust-andes

Organic Farming: http://en.wikipedia.org/wiki/International_Federation_of_Organic_Agriculture_Movements

Desertification:

Aral   Sea: http://www.columbia.edu/~tmt2120/environmental%20impacts.htm

Silent Crisis: http://www.ghf-ge.org/human-impact-report.pdf

Green Belt: http://www.greatgreenwall.org

http://www.greenbeltmovement.org/what-we-do/tree-planting-for-watersheds https://www.smithsonianmag.com/science-nature/great-green-wall-stop-desertification-not-so-much-180960171/

Rare Earth Metals: http://www.bbc.com/news/world-17357863

https://e360.yale.edu/features/a_scarcity_of_rare_metals_is_hindering_green_technologies

Waste and Garbage: https://cleantechnica.com/2013/08/26/us-wastes-61-86-of-its-energy/

Food Wastage: https://www.treehugger.com/green-investments/50-all-food-produced-wasted.html

Recycling statistics: http://prezi.com/rk2-zdjouqid/recycling-statistics/

Illegal Pollution: http://actionguide.info/t/11/

Hybrid cars: http://science.howstuffworks.com/science-vs-myth/everyday-myths/does-hybrid-car-production-waste-offset-hybrid-benefits1.htm

Chapter 5 - Flora

Phytoplankton:

http://faculty.bennington.edu/~sherman/the%20ocean%20project/the%20ocean's%20invisible%20forest.pdf http://www.scientificamerican.com/article/phytoplankton-population/

Algae:

http://www.engineering.com/DesignerEdge/DesignerEdgeArticles/ArticleID/7275/Microalgae-Lamp-Can-Absorb-One-Ton-of-Carbon-Per-Year.aspx

http://science.howstuffworks.com/environmental/green-science/algae-biodiesel.htm

Bees and Colony Collapse:

http://www.pbs.org/wnet/nature/episodes/silence-of-the-bees/impact-of-ccd-on-us-agriculture/37/

Rainforests: http://environment.about.com/od/healthenvironment/a/rainforest_drug.htm

QSMAS: http://cgspace.cgiar.org/bitstream/handle/10568/33607/4.6%20%20Conservation%20agriculture.pdf?sequence=1

Chapter 6 - Fauna

Fur Trade: http://www.furcommission.com/farming/production/

Dr. Temple Grandin: http://ww w.templegrandin.com/

Pets: http://www.factmonster.com/ipka/A0768602.html

Chapter 7 - Human Life

Philosophy and life: https://www.iep.utm.edu/mean-ana/

Philosophers on life: https://plato.stanford.edu/entries/life-meaning/

Begson on life: https://www.cairn.info/revue-internationale-de-philosophie-2007-3-page-287.htm#[4]

Heidegger on life: https://www.iep.utm.edu/heidegge/

Chapter 8 - Body – Brain

Nutrition thwarted: https://theblacksphere.net/2014/01/michelle-obamas-nutritious-lunch-program-failed/

GMOs and diseases: https://www.cittaslow.org/news/dramatic-correlation-shown-between-gmos-and-22-diseases

Pesticides in food: https://depts.washington.edu/ceeh/downloads/FF_Pesticides.pdf

Drugs: http://www.bu.edu/sjmag/scimag2005/features/drugsinwater.htm

Smoking – insomnia: https://www.everydayhealth.com/sleep/101/improve-sleep.aspx

Smoking – digestion: https://badgut.org/information-centre/a-z-digestive-topics/smoking-and-the-digestive-tract/

Voluntourism: http://www.albasud.org/noticia/en/1132/volunteer-tourists-which-are-their-motivations

over/undernutrition: https://www.verywellfit.com/understanding-malnutrition-2507055

---

4. https://www.cairn.info/revue-internationale-de-philosophie-2007-3-page-287.htm

Respecting elders: https://www.huffpost.com/entry/what-other-cultures-can-teach_n_4834228

Japan seniors: https://www.nytimes.com/2011/06/28/world/asia/28fukushima.html

Chapter 9 - Mind

Internet:

http://www.telegraph.co.uk/news/worldnews/europe/finland/3080834/School-shootings-Finnish-gunmen-plotted-death-sprees-together-online.html

Nun Study: http://www.wired.com/wiredscience/2009/07/nun-study/

http://compulsionsolutions.com/warning-to-parents-porn-on-xbox-via-youporn-by-compulsion-coach-craig-perra-jd/

http://www.paintthestateidaho.org/galleryView.php?id=199

http://methproject.org

http://www.wired.com/underwire/2009/07/penn-teller-call-bullshit-on-videogame-violence/

http://www.policyinnovations.org/ideas/briefings/data/000081

Videos

http://www.ted.com/talks/pw_singer_on_robots_of_war.html

http://www.youtube.com/watch?v=aMbWmZ7SG-c

Books

Norman S. Doidge, <u>The Brain That Changes Itself</u>

V.S. Ramachandran, <u>The Tell-Tale Brain</u>

David Snowdon, <u>Aging With Grace</u>

Movies/TV

"Moral Kombat," 2009: http://www.moralkombatmovie.com/

National Geographic, "World's Most Dangerous Drug," 2006: http://shop.nationalgeographic.com/ngs/product/dvds/adventure-and-exploration/world%27s-most-dangerous-drug-dvd, http://top-documentaryfilms.com/the-worlds-most-dangerous-drug/

Hashtags in Social Media

These hashtags are used to target relevant articles associated with the subjects in *Audit of the Universe*. In this way, we can have up-to-date information in our specific category of interest. These hashtags appear all over the internet, but more specifically on Facebook. A more extensive list is present on the site TheExplanation.com[1].

The idea is to build a library of trustworthy information available to researchers and students alike. Feel free to use these hashtags for articles of interest you find in your reading. Then, post them to Facebook and other social media so we can all take better stock of the state of our Planet.

1 #AuditSpace

Orbiting *space nation* data center could avoid all Earthly laws https://buff.ly/2vJHHmA #Laws control #international waters but not so in *space*. It's a *free-for-all* and some of taking advantage of this vacuum. Who does #space belong to? #theExplanation #AuditSpace

*****

Strange Stars Caught Wrinkling Spacetime? Get the Facts. https://buff.ly/2wJSQZq The technical stuff is well beyond me and, probably, you. However, the enormity of #stars, #neutrons, and gravitational waves should help us realize our position in the #Universe. #Humankind is, at the same time, *nothing* and *everything*. We are insignificant on a universal scale but so significant that we can #contemplate both the Universe and ourselves. Why is this so? #theExplanation #InventorySpace

---

2 #AuditAtmosphere #AuditClimate

Renewable Energy Record Set in U.S. http://buff.ly/2s3saBb Good news: We're making headway in renewable energy #theExplanation #AuditAtmosphere

*****

Living with climate change: What's the worst that can happen? http://buff.ly/2tUm1q9 #Climate #researchers worry that #melting of #Arctic and #Antarctic #ice may have passed its tipping point, beyond which #change feeds on itself and cannot be stopped. #theExplanation #AuditAtmosphere

*****

Three years to safeguard our climate http://buff.ly/2u50p95 Can it be done? Here are their three keys to #success: First, use #science to guide decisions and set targets. Second, existing #solutions must be scaled up rapidly. Third, encourage #optimism. We'll know by 2020 if the glass is getting fuller or emptier. #theExplanation #AuditClimate

*****

Carbon Dioxide Levels on Increase Worldwide. What's Happening? https://buff.ly/2x1s1ge Is the #COP 21 #climate agreement history or actuality? What is the state of affairs of #Earths #atmosphere? #theExplanation #AuditAtmosphere

3 #AuditWater

Turning point: Reef inspector http://buff.ly/2st9pXf Coral Reef endangerment due to bleaching is becoming an ecological disaster. The elephant in the room is climate change causing the water to heat up. Also, with increased seaside tourism, tons of sunscreen lotion with non-biodegradable elements wash into the sea and affect the algae food supply causing the coral to starve and turn white ... hence the name: coral bleaching.

*****

The fight to save thousands of lives with sea-floor sensors http://buff.ly/2v6vrgT #Technology to detect and transmit #underwater land movement has made incredible progress. However, consider a massive ocean-floor fault just 50km from a densely populated shoreline. We don't know when we're waiting, but this is much bigger than #sensors. #theExplanation #AuditWater

*****

Air guns used in offshore oil exploration can kill tiny marine life http://buff.ly/2vtw3N5 #zooplankton killed off, commercial #fish species endangered. Maybe we need #oil, but we also need fish. The dilemma is needing both when the obtention of one obliterates the other. What do you do? #theExplanation #AuditWater

4 #AuditLand #AuditPollution #AuditResources #AuditEcology #AuditEnvironment

Govern land as a global commons http://buff.ly/2sKf07W We've reached a crossroads in world population and land use for #agriculture[2]. Where next? #theExplanation[3] #AuditLand

---

2. https://www.facebook.com/hashtag/agriculture

*****

The Vittel Case https://buff.ly/2iKdeno Vittel proves that changing agricultural practices benefits both the economy and individual lives. #theExplanation #AuditLand

*****

Developing countries: Growing threat of urban waste dumps http://buff.ly/2t5JWCF By 2025, it will be enough to fill a line of #rubbish trucks 5,000 kilometers long every day; this is a real down-to-conundrum. Some #cities have made great #progress to improve, but globally who is facing this issue? #theExplanation #AuditPollution

*****

A Running List of How Trump Is Changing the Environment https://buff.ly/2v8mgMoThe Explanation is not the only one doing an #Audit of the #Environment. #NationalGeographic has always done it and is scrutinizing the #Trump administration. Read on; the picture reveals that the glass of peace and prosperity is getting emptier. #theExplanation #AuditEnvironment

*****

Explaining the Deadly Sierra Leone Mudslide https://buff.ly/2vk-bGS0 #Deforestation taking place on hilltops, clogged drainages, and the removal of #mangroves are factors likely to contribute to future #flooding and #mudslides. We don't see tree roots, but they hold #topsoil and #earth together. Is the glass of environmental care getting fuller or emptier? #theExplanation #AuditLand

---

3. https://www.facebook.com/hashtag/theexplanation

5 #AuditFlora

Biodiversity moves beyond counting species http://buff.ly/2rRTFMD
Another breakthrough, #biodiversity[4] is even more than the *richness of traits*. It is interconnectivity at the highest level. You can generally read a word by recognizing its consonants, but adding some, most, or all of the vowels make it complete. Similarly, with biodiversity. Have biologists reached the stage where they can identify all the 'traits' in a given species? Certainly, there are *lesser influences,* but #ecology[5] is the interconnectivity of the whole, all the various elements in an ecosystem. #theExplanation[6] #AuditFlora[7]

*****

Italy rebuked for failure to prevent olive-tree tragedy https://buff.ly/2vEZKLF Some environmentalists fight researchers over the cause of dying #olive trees. the #environmentalists have also stopped the felling of diseased trees which is an effort to stop the progress of the infection into Northern Italy. While the judicial crisis deepens, the disease makes further inroads into Italy and other areas in Europe. #theExplanation #AuditFlora

*****

Reassess dam building in the Amazon http://buff.ly/2svDjdJ This article says: The framework avoids the common pitfall of evaluating each dam in isolation. It's not just #dams. Have we forgotten that everything ... and I mean everything to do with our planet, within the Universe, is connected. It's a puzzle with all the pieces assembled ... perfectly. It's

---

4. https://www.facebook.com/hashtag/biodiversity

5. https://www.facebook.com/hashtag/ecology

6. https://www.facebook.com/hashtag/theexplanation

7. https://www.facebook.com/hashtag/auditflora

coherent completeness. With 17% of the world's fresh #water supplies, the #Amazon is a huge reservoir. What are we doing? #theExplanation #Auditwater #Auditflora

*****

UN Announces 23 New Nature Reserves While the U.S. Removes 17 https://buff.ly/2vEsBzH #Biosphere reserves are areas comprising terrestrial, marine, and coastal #ecosystems and are designated "learning places" for testing different #sustainable approaches. http://buff.ly/2taTsWs Mankind is becoming more aware of and trying to learn more about its environment ... and do something about preserving it. #theExplanation #AuditFlora

*****

The Plant Paradox: Are All Vegetables Good for Us? http://buff.ly/2tHBhru Healthy diets are not easy to come by, more controversy. But, Flora is the mainstay of all vibrant life ... amazing how it's an important piece in the inventory and Audit of our Earth. #theExplanation #AuditFlora

*****

Aboriginal fire management https://buff.ly/2utkdST #Ancestral #knowledge can be better than #contemporary knowledge. Being the boss of the #fire was always the way. NOT fire being the boss of us, that's the #lesson from the old #people. #theExplanation #AuditFlora

6. #AuditFauna

Two-Headed Porpoise Found For First Time http://buff.ly/2t6xyCS Unnatural sea creatures. What could be the cause? This one couldn't be examined ... but is it the result of humankind's effect on our oceans? #theExplanation #Auditfauna

*****

Biological annihilation via the ongoing sixth mass extinction signaled by vertebrate population losses and declines https://buff.ly/2wSdjZ3 We emphasize that the sixth mass #extinction is already here and the window for effective action is probably two or three decades at most. All signs point to ever more powerful #assaults on #biodiversity in the next two decades, painting a dismal picture of the future of #life, including #human life. #theExplanation #AuditFauna

*****

Ocean Life Eats Tons of Plastic—Here's Why That Matters https://buff.ly/2x7WrNT #Humankind has turned the world's #oceans into what #scientists call a "plastic soup." And guess who the end #consumer of this soup is? You and me. We're chewing on our own #garbage. #theExplanation #AuditFauna #AuditPollution

1. #AuditLife

Frequency dependence limits divergent #evolution by favoring rare immigrants over residents http://buff.ly/2rpQdVN This is a concise introduction to a complex aspect of evolution. My opinion is that you can't know if one plus one is going to equal two. More complexity to an already complex subject. #theExplanation #AuditLife

1. #AuditHumanBody

New concerns raised over value of #genome-wide disease studies http://buff.ly/2uxz5QJ This article states: These *peripheral* #DNA variants probably act through complex biochemical regulatory networks to influence the activity of a few 'core' #genes that are more directly connected to an illness. It's time to realize how complex the body is and how #plasticity plays a role in making each human an individuality. #theExplanation #AuditBody

9 #AuditBrainMind #AuditBrain #AuditMind

The Most Effective Psychotherapy For Borderline Personality http://buff.ly/2te28rv The best way to deal with #mental #disorders. Why is the #mind preponderant with #humankind? The way to prepare and work with the mind is primordial. #theExplanation #AuditMind

*****

"Better Care" Could Mean No Care https://buff.ly/2wFMo2u The positive side is our awareness of this debilitating situation. #Mental #disorders are not only quite common but also quite impairing. Mental #illness has become the last #frontier for #human rights. The mind is central to #humankind's #welfare. #theExplanation #AuditMind

*****

The Cognitive Audit https://buff.ly/2uFYyqO With a job, #profession, #career, one's #skills, #training, and #knowledge are important but how one's #mind adapts to new or unexpected circumstances is beyond what we are prepared for. Why and how does the mind adapt to #changing situations? #theExplanation #AuditMind #AuditHumanSingularity

*****

New Research Confirms 9 Ways to Help Beat Dementia https://buff.ly/2xzsE0a Lifestyle #health is important, but the keys are elsewhere. #Cognitive stimulation and creative activities. #Social contact via group activity. Why are #humans so dependant on their #minds and '#neighbors?' #theExplanation #AuditMind

*****

Coping With Not Knowing What Happened to a #Missing #LovedOne http://buff.ly/2toJeie #Hope can be a support when there's #mental turmoil, but hope for what? #theExplanation #AuditMind

*****

We can't ban killer robots – it's already too late | Philip Ball https://buff.ly/2gaxOfB #Chemical #warfare, atomic warfare, anti-personnel mines ... all developed technology that (most) nations have outlawed because of their deadliness. Now come #killerrobots commanded only by their own #algorhithm. They choose their own #targets and can #kill indiscriminately. Why can #human minds develop such atrocities? #theExplanation #AuditMind #AuditViolence

www.TheExplanation.com

Join The Explanation Newsletter[8], no spam, total privacy

Sam's latest blog post notifications and information about The Explanation

---

8. https://mailchi.mp/theexplanation/7keystomasterbiblicalhebrew

Don't miss out!

Visit the website below and you can sign up to receive emails whenever Sam Kneller publishes a new book. There's no charge and no obligation.

https://books2read.com/r/B-A-GZZJ-WQZEB

BOOKS 2 READ

Connecting independent readers to independent writers.

Also by Sam Kneller

Watch for more at https://www.TheExplanation.com.

About the Author

SAM KNELLER was born in London and has lived in the United Kingdom, South Africa, Spain, Canada, Israel, Belgium, and for the past forty years in France. After spending twenty-five years in the Christian ministry, Sam taught website creation at the American University in Paris.

He also worked as a technical writer and founded BonjourLaFrance.com, a successful site for travel and tourism in France. All the while delving into Biblical Hebrew and the Bible in preparation for this series of books about Genesis and God's Plan.

He is currently occupied with webmastering, studying, teaching, and writing his weekly blog TheExplanation.com

Read more at https://www.TheExplanation.com.

www.ingramcontent.com/pod-product-compliance
Lightning Source LLC
Chambersburg PA
CBHW020314290526
45785CB00007B/2786

* 9 7 8 1 3 9 3 0 3 5 3 0 5 *